D1202716

CHAMPIONS
FOREVER

ACKNOWLEDGEMENTS

I dedicate this book to each and everyone of my former athletes. Despite the times of trial, frustration, disappointment, and tears, they helped make my life worth living. The joys, surprises, friendships, and togetherness enriched my life in so many ways. I just loved every one of them. Their cheery "Hi Coach" brought a little bit of Heaven each time. Thank you fellows for being my friends.

All incidents in this book are true, and God involved the author in each one. However, the author has sought to protect the identity of those referred to in this book, except where permission has been given. Otherwise, names have been changed.

This book was not written to degrade any individual or groups of individuals. I told it as it was, but with no intent to be critical of any individual. I loved and respected every school board member, administrator, teacher, coach, parent, student, athlete, and official, with whom I was associated. I praise God for each one of them.

I praise God for the communities of Williamston, Michigan and Coldwater, Michigan. These two communities were so good to me and my family. How fortunate I feel to have had the opportunity of serving them. It was wonderful!

CHAMPIONS FOREVER

by Coach Floyd Eby

PUBLISHED AND PRINTED BY EAGLE PRINTING CO., INC.
COLDWATER, MICHIGAN

FIRST PRINTING - SEPTEMBER, 1978

OTHER BOOKS BY THE AUTHOR
CALLING GOD'S TOWER...COME IN, PLEASE!
MIRACLES OF LOVE

CONTENTS

Acknowledgements

About The Author

Preface

Introduction

Chapter 1	*A New Coach Survives*	21
Chapter 2	*The Birth of "Race Horse" Basketball, The Zone Full Court Press, The One Handed Jump Shot, And The One-Two-Two Basic Zone*	28
Chapter 3	*Attempting To Escape*	44
Chapter 4	*The Stranger In Town*	54
Chapter 5	*The Birth of Split T Football And The Open Huddle*	65
Chapter 6	*The Creation Of A Basketball Dynasty*	87
Chapter 7	*Back To Reality And Humility*	109
Chapter 8	*Trials, Tribulations, And The Blessings Of A Coach*	125
Chapter 9	*A New Football Regime*	148
Chapter 10	*A Tough Brand of Discipline ...Headline-Making Sports*	167
Chapter 11	*An Exciting New Life - My Own Testimony*	204
Chapter 12	*How To Come Alive*	218

ABOUT THE AUTHOR

"ON THE WINNING TEAM"

Coach Floyd Eby pictured with his 1949 State Basketball Championship Team of Coldwater High School of Coldwater, Michigan.

The team members now include two dentists, an ordained minister, a teacher and coach, two high ranking Army Officers, a pharmacist, a university science instructor, two outstanding business executives and three successful businessmen.

Coach Eby pictured below as he appears now in serving His Lord Jesus full time as speaker, evangelist, missionary, lay witness, counselor, and Gideon distributing the Word of God. Coach Eby also holds Bible studies in homes. Coach Floyd Eby has a wife, Betty, two daughters and four grandchildren.

Coach Floyd Eby has been credited by many coaches and fans as the orginator of the basketball full court zone press, "race horse" basketball, and the one handed jump shot as early as 1939. Coach Eby was also the originator of the football open huddle, defensive huddle and the split T offense. God has guided Coach Eby into many endeavors: 1.) Master of Science degree plus ten credits toward a Doctorate from Michigan State University at East Lansing, Michigan.
2.) Taught Science 30 years in the secondary public schools

of Michigan. Selected Teacher of the Year in the State of Michigan in 1965.

3.) Coached 25 years as head coach in basketball, and other sports such as football, baseball, and track for a lesser number of years. The coaching career included many championships, including two State Championships in basketball, but even more important included so many opportunities to witness for his Saviour to so many young people.

4.) State President of the Michigan Gideons for three years.

5.) Two years overseas in the United States Navy during World War Two as Communications Officer on a Destroyer Escort.

6.) He flies his own plane approximately 60,000 miles per year, and the Lord has given him the opportunity to give over 200 messages each year including athletic banquets, church banquets, Junior and Senior high schools, college groups, pulpit supply and Gideon messages throughout the midwest.

7.) He has also been engaged in many business enterprises: Cablevision, Building Contracting Business, Modular Homes, Mobile Homes, Financing, Sub-division, Insurance, Real Estate, Sports Announcer, and Frozen Foods. The above made it possible for him to serve his Lord, and pay his own way with funds supplied by his Lord through the above enterprises.

8.) He has also had the opportunity to work with over 3000 people in the Midwest and other states: telling about God's wonderful plan for their lives, seeing them join the Family of God, and then follow-up with them with visits, letters and phone calls, as well as home Bible studies to encourage them to grow spiritually. He has over 3000 people on his prayer list.

9.) Selected for State High School Coaches Hall of Fame in 1964.

10.) Elected Outstanding Citizen of Coldwater, Michigan, his home town, in 1976 by the Greater Coldwater Area Chamber of Commerce.

11.) Author of book, *"Calling God's Tower, Come in Please."*

CHAMPIONS FOREVER

Preface

Floyd Eby is a natural story-teller who writes just as he talks, unfettered by grammar or other literary restrictions. He offers no philosophic rationalizations; no fancy words; no apologies. He writes in plain, simple, straight-from-the-shoulder language that cuts through even exceedingly complex subjects, making you wonder why anyone ever got it so tangled up in the first place.

That's the way he wrote his first book, *Calling God's Tower -- Come In, Please!* It's the only way you would ever want Floyd Eby to write. It may be a literary aberration, if you weigh it by grammatical accuracy, sentence construction, syntax, or on any other common scale of literary consideration. But there is an undeniable sincerity; a direct, uncluttered approach to Floyd Eby's writing that comes through, grabbing both mental and emotional responses, culminating finally in a total reading experience that transcends the crossing of t's and the dotting of i's.

Champions Forever will be enjoyed by anyone who has ever been involved in athletics, either as a coach or as an athlete. It offers both a contrast and a parallel between athletics in the 1940's and today.

And Coach Floyd Eby is imminently qualified -- as much as any man of this century -- to talk about high school coaching.

Because Coach Eby was more than a coach. He was an innovator in athletics, creating without realizing it some of the classic plays that have come about in both basketball and football. "You have to make the most of what you have," is his only statement about such innovations as race-horse basketball, the one-handed jump shot, the full court zone press, the split-T and the open huddle in football (see newspaper stories about Floyd Eby, in the back of this book); all his own creations.

Beyond his inventiveness in athletics, Coach Floyd Eby has

won the respect, admiration, and affection of the citizens in the area where he lives -- those less likely to be impressed by single acts, but who are directly affected by a total person.

Coach Floyd Eby presents 1956 Twin Valley League Sportsmanship Trophy to Principal Kermit Dennis while high school Mayor Roland Peterson looks on. This trophy is awarded for the sportsmanlike conduct of athletes, fans, and staff. The honor was bestowed on the school several times while Coach Eby headed the athletic program.

Floyd was awarded the single highest honor his community could give him in 1976, when he was voted Outstanding Citizen by the Greater Coldwater Area Chamber of Commerce. This came on top of numerous honors in athletics, including two state champion basketball teams -- one from Coldwater, and one from Williamston, Michigan.

Coach Floyd Eby has touched the lives of literally thousands of people through his personal ministry, by carrying the word of Jesus Christ to every corner of the country, often flying his own airplane, always at his own expense, "Wherever my Lord wants me to serve."

Shortly after his first book was published, a reporter from Associated Press called the publishers and wanted to know, "What's the catch?" with Coach Floyd Eby.

There's no "catch" with Floyd Eby, the reporter was told. Later, after the reporter read *Calling God's Tower -- Come In, Please!*, his cynicism vanished and he wrote one of the best reviews the book was to receive. And, in less than three years, it was to sell almost 40,000 copies -- a monumental testimony to an uncommonly decent man.

If you have ever wondered what you could get out of athletics, or if you have ever pondered the question of what athletics did for you, *Champions Forever* will give you the answer.

If you are a coach, were one, or are about to be one, you will enjoy every page of *Champions Forever*.

Even if you were never involved in athletics, this book has an important message for you.

Robert Charles
Publisher

INTRODUCTION

*"And let us not get tired of
doing what is right, for after
a while we will reap a harvest
of blessing if we don't get
discouraged and give up."*
Galatians 6:9

While I cannot say that God spoke to me and said, "Floyd
Eby, I want you to be a coach," the more I think about it, He
might as well have. Because from the time I was in junior
high school, that's what I wanted to be. It didn't occur to me
then that is what the Lord wanted me to be.

I was an excellent football player, for my size, if I do say
so, particularly in high school. I was good in college, too, but
those bigger guys brought me down to size. Frankly, I just
wasn't big enough for college football. And I wasn't very
good at any other sport besides football. And maybe because
I couldn't perform all that well myself, that's why I wanted to
coach. I could have the thrill of winning, through what I
would teach others.

Certainly, at the time I began coaching, it did not occur to
me that I was accepting what I now know is the most
challenging of all callings, the call to teach.

Our Lord, Jesus Christ, was of course the greatest teacher
of all. Only He had to teach under the threat of losing His
life, what with Roman soldiers hanging around, ready to
crush this "rabble rouser" like a fly, at a moment's notice.
All we coaches had to lose was our jobs.

Our Lord turned over an enormous amount of wonderful
and powerful opportunities to me as a coach, to teach not
only physical fitness but to teach a total way of life that can
be the closest parallel there is to a life of Christianity. And
there were few strings attached. There were no Roman
soldiers.

And aside from the downtown quarterbacks who wanted a
winning team above all else, and some of the parents who
couldn't understand what I was trying to do, and a few of the
athletes' girl friends whose occasional selfishness could

sometimes cause training rules to be broken, and aside from some of the athletes themselves who wouldn't understand me until years afterwards, there were few limits to my opportunities.

While the Lord knew what He was doing when He got me into coaching, I didn't fully realize it until my career was more than half way finished. Then I must confess there were moments when I wondered if the Lord really knew what he was doing, and I thought maybe He had made an enormous mistake.

One of my former coaches who is now an Athletic Director, said not long ago that the athletic departments of high schools are "the last bastions of discipline" left in schools today. Unfortunately, there is a great deal of truth to what he said, and it is a sad commentary on our times. But as I write this I see signs of some of the old-fashioned discipline, such as they had when I taught, returning to our high schools. And I don't think the kids are going to be upset by it as much as some of the parents and teachers fear they might be.

It can be argued that we now have the best athletes in the world, so why return to more discipline in high schools. My feeling has always been that we are doing more than turning out better athletes through the training we give them in high school. We are turning out better total individuals. You just can't do it, in my opinion, when each kid is allowed to do his own thing, when, and however he pleases. The kids don't even respect us for allowing such nonsense. Young people, when you really get to know them, want to know what is expected of them. It's up to teachers and responsible adults to let them know, and to help them achieve the best they can with what they have.

Teenagers are no worse today than ever. If youth are worse today, it is because they have been mishandled by adults including teachers, coaches, and parents.

I sincerely believe the most important qualification of a teacher and a coach is love for their students or athletes. I believe that each one can sense our love for them. This does not mean that we are not to be strict at times in our handling of students and athletes. The strictness must be tempered with the love of Jesus. Each time I was forced to "chew" out a student or athlete, I would make a point of treating them extra nice the very next time I met them. This would take the edge off after our mission had been accomplished.

Students and athletes have to like a teacher or a coach in order for the teacher or coach to influence their lives. However, lack of discipline does not produce the relationship to bring about influence for good. Even in this day I believe students and athletes can be disciplined if the teacher or coach is firm, fair, and consistent, and administers the rules in the love of Jesus. Every student and athlete is as important as the other, whether they are gifted or not, super star or not.

I always made it a point to visit all of my students who missed five consecutive days in one week. I would visit them on that weekend to see if I could be of any help. Every athlete in school, star or scrub who was hospitalized was visited no matter what squad he was on. I did this because I loved them and I loved them because Jesus first loved me. My students and athletes did more for me than I did for them.

Not very many young people can be champions in athletics. But all young people can become champions with their lives --- they can become champions for a lifetime --- if we as adults give them a chance, and give them proper guidance.

How did we handle athletes in the "old days"? What did we do that was so different? What was it like to be a coach? What was it like to be an athlete in a small high school in a small town in the late 30's and 40's? Many people ask me these questions, particularly young people on high school and college campuses, once they learn that I was a coach.

"Coach Eby," they ask, "what was it like, back then?"

This book is for the young people of all ages who ask now, and may ask later, what high school athletics was like during the 1940's. Of course I can only tell it as one person, as one coach, saw it.

The author has convenanted with his Lord, that all monies

derived from the sale of this book will be used one hundred per cent in the Missionary Work of our Lord Jesus Christ. God has already taken care of his daily needs.

If God has in some way used this book to help you, either as an unbeliever becoming a believer, or as a believer becoming strengthened in the faith, or as a believer being used of God in telling others; the author invites you to write to him or telephone him and he will put you on his prayer list. If you send a picture of yourself, the author will put it on his prayer board.

The author will also try to visit you as his Lord opens the door, and makes time available. There is absolutely no cost or obligation to any of the above, as it has already been paid for by the atoning blood of Jesus on the Cross. May our Lord bless you as you read this book. All correspondence to be mailed to:

Floyd Eby
15 Cardinal Drive
Coldwater, Michigan 49036
Phone 517-278-5031

Unworthy but His,
Coach Floyd Eby

LEFT TO RIGHT: COACH WILLIAM ZABONICK, COACH EBY AND COACH FRED HOBART. Coaches Zabonick and Hobart played for Coach Eby at Coldwater High School. Both excelled at several sports. After graduation from high school both Bill and Fred became all conference athletes. Bill at Western Michigan University and Fred at Adrian College. Later Bill and Fred were on the Coldwater coaching staff with Coach Eby. Bill has been the very successful head basketball coach at Bronson High School for many years. At the same time Fred has produced many winners as the Coldwater High School head basketball coach after taking over for Coach Eby when he retired in 1964. Both Bill and Fred have taken their basketball teams to the "big time" in the STATE TOURNEY SEMI-FINALS. When Coldwater plays Bronson, Coach Eby is in a dilemma. He wants to "root" for both teams.

*"I have fought a good fight, I
have finished my course, I have
kept the faith"*
2 Timothy 4:7

1

A NEW COACH SURVIVES

I blew my whistle, and shouted.

"Come on in guys, come on in now."

No one paid any attention to me. This was my first night of football practice on my new job. This was really "cold turkey." I did not know one player on this team. Some were throwing the football around. Others were kicking it. Some were wrestling on the ground; some were sun-bathing on the ground, some were arguing, and some were pretending to be sleeping. But no one was paying any attention to me.

Once again I blew my whistle long and hard, and shouted much louder this time.

"Come on in guys, we need to get started now."

Still no one even looked my way. They completely ignored me. I was stumped. I wondered if my alma mater, Michigan State University, hadn't really goofed up on my training and education to be a high school coach. I couldn't remember one course that had covered this particular situation.

* * *

I graduated from Michigan State in the spring of 1939 as a Physical Education Major with a major in science. My degree stated that I was qualified to coach all sports and teach many various subjects. However, the United States was just coming out of the depression and jobs were very scarce. In fact, unless you had previous teaching and coaching experience, your chances of getting a coaching and teaching job were practically nil.

Only four out of twenty-two Physical Education Majors graduating from Michigan State that spring secured jobs. I was one of the other eighteen. I had gone back to Michigan State to work on a Smith Hughes degree to qualify to teach Agriculture in the secondary schools. There seemed to be a need in that area.

As I was attending classes on the campus in September, I received a call from the college placement office.

Williamston High School in Williamston, Michigan, was in need of a head football coach. Williamston was a high school only about thirteen miles east of the college campus on Grand River. The school was used as a student training institution for the college.

School at Williamston had been in session for four weeks. The board had hired a new football coach from Ohio who had started football practice on Labor Day. His name was Duke. Duke after four short weeks was the idol of the entire community. Everybody loved Duke, the townspeople, parents, and students. He had installed a football system in four short weeks that had impressed the team, school, and town. Williamston swamped their opening opponent, and this added to Duke's already high popularity rating.

At this time Michigan State, my alma mater, became the "villain" in the great happenings that were taking place at Williamston High School under the tutelage of the lovable Duke. Michigan State approved the hiring of all teachers who were to handle student teachers from the college. All supervising teachers were required to have a Masters Degree. Duke had claimed to have a Masters Degree. He was short, having stretched the truth by only a few credits.

When Michigan State carefully checked the records, they found this error. They immediately served the Williamston School Board with the ultimatum of firing Duke or lose all their student teachers from the college. At this time the money that the college was paying Williamston for the training of their practicing teachers was an integral part of the Williamston School Budget. They could not operate without it.

The school board notified the college that there was no way that they could fire their beloved Duke. The college held firm and demanded his release or else lose this money. The School Board reluctantly gave in and released Duke.

Leonard, the superintendent, became temporary head football coach. Duke did not leave town but continued to ready his team for the second game with Stockbridge. During the game, Leonard sat on the bench with the team but Duke raced up and down the sidelines making substitutions and calling the plays.

Stockbridge was crushed 26-0, and Duke's popularity soared. Michigan State was hated by all, for trying to get rid of their great coach. However, Michigan State insisted that Duke had to leave town which he finally did. This seemed to infuriate the team members, students, and townspeople.

Students and their parents picketed the school. They paraded the town carrying signs: "We want Duke," "Down with Michigan State," "Spartans back to East Lansing where you belong," "Bring Duke back," "Kick the student teachers out."

They insisted that the school board stand up for the community's rights. Williamston students when asked questions in classes by Michigan State student teachers would not answer. If the teacher insisted on the student answering the question, the student would just answer, "We want Duke."

The situation was so critical that an experienced coach would not consider the position. Therefore the Williamston School Board wanted to interview anyone who would consider the job. The position had to be filled quickly regardless of the results.

I drove to Williamston for an interview with the Superintendent. Leonard was a kindly man and very gracious. He explained the entire problem to me as sort of a warning, if I was hired to succeed Duke.

Leonard gave me the names of the three school board members and told me where I could locate them. He asked me to go look them up and discuss the position with each one of them. I realized the critical nature of the job I was seeking, but I really didn't care. I was fed up with going to College. I wanted to get out and make some money, and a name for myself.

I wasn't concerned with the fact that it would be almost impossible to succeed in this type of coaching and teaching situation. Especially with no experience. And if I failed in my first coaching job, I knew I would probably never secure another job. But I decided that I was going to go all out to get this job, regardless of what happened to my career.

First of all I contacted Mr. Smith, the owner of the local shoe store. After talking shoes for awhile, I tried to sell myself as the man who could do the job.

I then drove over to the railroad depot, and introduced myself to Mr. Cody, the president of the school board and a railroad man. After discussing freight and passenger trains, I indicated to Mr. Cody my desire to obtain the coaching and teaching position that Williamston had open.

From the depot I drove south of town to meet Mr. Jones at his farm. This was much more down my line than shoes and railroads, as I was brought up on the farm. Mr. Jones and I had a fine discussion on the needs of the school in this particular area at this time.

The next day, on Wednesday, Leonard the superintendent called me. He asked me to come out to his office, which I anxiously did. Leonard told me that he and the school board had decided to try me in filling the position vacated by Duke. He offered me a contract, which I signed immediately.

The center on the football team, Sam, stepped into the office, and Leonard introduced me to him. I stuck my hand

out and said, "Hello." Sam refused to shake hands with me.
Sam said it was no use of me coming in and trying to straighten matters out. It was not going to work.

However, I made my way down to the locker-room and dressed. I walked out to the football field to meet the squad and to hold my first football practice.

The team had been practicing by itself since Duke had left town, and practice was under the control of Captain Len. All week the team members had been fighting, swearing, and doing just as they pleased. Even Captain Len was chewing tobacco and spitting in some of their faces as a joke, while others were entertaining themselves in various other ways.

* * *

After blowing the whistle the second time and shouting for the players to come on in with no results whatsoever, I blew the whistle as loud and long as I could.

I shouted as loud as I could shout.

"I am giving all of you just thirty seconds to come and talk with me, and those who don't are as of now officially cut from this squad!"

Captain Len started slowly moving towards me. I could hear him say: "Come on guys, we'll see what this guy has to say." Some started coming up to face me while others on the ground just rolled over towards me, and others came on all fours. Some sat down on the ground. Others stood.

All were looking at me with suspicion, contempt, and hatred. After all, this new coach was a graduate of hated Michigan State, the institution responsible for the firing of their beloved Duke.

One thing I knew was that I had better say the right words or my career would be over before it ever started.

"Fellows, I am truly sorry for the situation that we find ourselves in. However, it is not your fault, and no way am I to blame for it. The fact is that this critical situation exists and you and I need to do something about it. I cannot replace your good coach Duke and you have no way of bringing him back. I know Duke is an excellent coach, and it is too bad that he had to leave.

"There is only one way that you and I can show this school and this community, and Michigan State what an outstanding coach Duke really is. That is by winning the rest of our football games. To do this we need to become a team of harmony. Then we can finish what Duke started by having Duke's team go undefeated."

As I spoke I watched the different players. I could see it was making sense to most of them. After all this new coach admitted he wasn't the coach that Duke was. This new coach wanted to give Duke the credit for an undefeated team.

So practice finally got underway on that Wednesday afternoon. We were to play Leslie on Friday, and Okemos the following Wednesday, because of Teachers' Institute on the following Thursday and Friday. We had two tough games in six days. I had to learn all the plays that Duke had taught them. There was no time for me to teach my system and plays. Fortunately Duke was a good coach and had taught the team well. He had developed a good system, both on offense and defense. I had to drop one illegal play, but I approved all the others.

Even though most of the players were suspicious of me, most of them started cooperating. After about an hour and a half of scrimmage and running plays, I dismissed practice. The players trotted into the locker-room and I walked after them by myself.

Before I arrived at the locker-room door I was surrounded by 25 to 30 young kids, most of them 5th to 8th graders. They surrounded me and escorted me to the locker-room. They threw stones and sticks at me, cursed me, and called me all kinds of names. They expressed how much they hated me and Michigan State. They shouted that I had better leave town, and let Duke come back. I tried as best I could to ignore their insults, and duck the thrown sticks and stones. I finally broke loose and ran into the locker-room and shut them out.

I had just about had it. I was ready to break down and bawl. I just didn't know what to do with small kids like that.

There was no way I could retaliate. I went back to my room at Michigan State and worked hard learning all the new plays, and planning my strategy for Thursday's practice and Friday's game at Leslie.

Another major problem arose. I knew that the superstar, Ron, had not been at practice on Wednesday. I looked him up in school on Thursday. "I understand, Ron, that you have quit the team," I said. "Oh no, coach," he replied. "I have some bad ribs. I won't be ready until game time."

"If you are not out for practice tonight, Ron, I am cutting you for the season," I said, as I walked away.

Ron showed up for Thursday's practice. So did the rest of the squad. Most of the squad was now treating me much better than the general student body, because I had bragged up their wonderful Duke.

Now I knew that my career hinged on the winning of the next two ball games. It looked like it would take a miracle.

On Friday afternoon at Leslie, we were behind 12 to 7. With two minutes to go, we had 3rd down and eight on the thirty yard line. Dunckel threw a long pass to Gaffner, our right end. Dean ran seventy yards for a touchdown to win the game 13 to 12. Thank God for a miracle.

We had only Monday and Tuesday to get ready for Okemos.

Wednesday, at Okemos, we were behind 6 to 0 in the last quarter. Ron got loose on a long run and we won 7 to 6.

After the Okemos game, I had ten days to prepare my team for the next game.

By that time we were prepared mentally, psychologically, and physically. I also had time to incorporate some of my own plays and ideas into Duke's system. From then on, no one came close to our team.

We went undefeated, finishing the season with a 46 to 0 romp over nearby rival Fowlerville. By now Duke had been pretty well forgotten, and everyone seemed to be 100 percent behind the team and their new coach. At least for the football season. Basketball was to provide an opportunity of a lifetime.

"For with God nothing shall be impossible"
Luke 1:37

2

THE BIRTH OF "RACE HORSE" BASKETBALL, THE ZONE FULL COURT PRESS, THE ONE HANDED JUMP SHOT, AND THE ONE-TWO-TWO BASIC ZONE.

My five foot, eight inch guard, Dick, came dribbling down the side of the great mammoth field house court. As he dribbled past me near the center of that large college court, I shouted at him, "Shoot it, Dick, shoot it, Dick."

Just as Dick let go of the ball, I thought: "What a stupid coach you are, Eby. Don't you know that Dick is the worst shot in the whole school. We have girls that can shoot better than Dick --- and here you are ordering him to take the most important shot of the season!"

Williamston High School was playing for the state basketball championship back in 1940 against Keego Harbor in Jenison Field House at Michigan State University in East Lansing, Michigan. I was fortunate to be the Williamston basketball coach at the time. Keego Harbor had won 57 out of 59 games over a three year period, and had an excellent team. However, with some new innovations in basketball, such as the zone full court press, fast break and race horse basketball, and the one-handed jump shot, we had worked our way into the finals.

At half-time against Keego Harbor, we had a 25 to 11 lead. A fourteen point lead might not sound like much, but at that time, it was the same as a thirty point lead today. I knew if we continued to play the type of ball we played the first half that we would have our first state championship.

As our players trooped into the locker room for the half-time recess, I saw them staring at those large championship trophies. I knew that I needed to keep their minds off the score and the big lead we had. I talked rapidly about improvements needed for the second half.

The locker room door opened. A photographer rushed in and exclaimed, "Coach, let me take a picture of the next state champions!"

I turned that photographer around and booted him right through that locker room door.

I could tell by the expressions on my players' faces that the damage had been done. I never did see the photographer again, but he must have been from Keego Harbor. As the second half was ending, Keego Harbor came down and made a shot that tied the game at 35 all.

A large round basketball scoreboard was being used in Jenison Field House. For the last minute of play the scoreboard would turn red, and after the last sixty seconds the board would turn white and the game would be over. When Keego Harbor tied the game up at 35 all, I looked up at the scoreboard. It was red and indicated 42 seconds left.

At this point Dick had cut the ball loose from the center of that large court on the orders of his coach. The basket looked miles away as compared to our small court in Williamston.

Dick was a marvelous defensive player, passer, play-maker, and rebounder, but he just couldn't shoot. All year long I had been forbidding him to shoot. Each game as our team would leave the locker room to go on the court, I would remind Dick, "Don't you shoot that ball, Dick, don't you dare shoot it. You let Wally and Ron shoot it. Do you understand?"

"Yeh, Coach, I understand," Dick would answer.

My story would end now, if I could tell you he made that shot from the center of the court and won the game. But he didn't. He missed as usual.

Keego Harbor picked off the rebound, dribbled it down the court, and worked it around our zone defense until they got it to their deadeye set shot. This player never seemed to miss when he had enough time. And we gave him too much time.

But praise God, he missed it.

Keego Harbor snatched their own rebound and passed it back out and started working it around. Once again their deadeye zeroed in a set shot. I knew that time had to be out. I expected the sound of the gun at any moment.

Fortunately he missed once again.

Dick jumped up in the air above the rim and snatched the ball off of that defensive board with his strong hands, and started dribbling down the same path once again -- right past me.

But by this time I had really smartened up, and I yelled, "Shoot it, Dick, shoot it, Dick!"

The same orders, and Dick is still the worst shot in the state.

And Dick once again let it go from the center of the court.

The ball went up, up, up toward the ceiling of that large arena, and then started on its way down. The ball hit the backboard and zipped through the net!

I looked up at that large round scoreboard, and it was still red. As I looked at it, the board turned white, and the game was officially over, and we had won the state championship.

However, it seemed as if I was the only person out of thirteen thousand screaming and screeching people that knew it. No one could hear the gun at the scorer's table. The players and officials kept going up and down the court playing the game. I rushed out on the court in my suit and tie, and started chasing the ball. The third time down the court I got the ball, and we were still ahead. We won!

I had been afraid that Keego Harbor would score a three point play and through a misunderstanding at the scorer's table we would lose the state championship. This was the first year that Williamston High School had ever won even a district championship, and this year we went all the way.

Even though our home was only twelve miles from East Lansing, we were staying in a Lansing Hotel, because the State was paying our expenses. The next morning, the team and I climbed out of bed to prepare to go back to Williamston and attend one of our local churches as a team.

I bought a Lansing State Journal.

There on the front page was my picture with large headlines, "Boy coaching wonder wins state championship in first year of coaching."

On the second page was a picture of Governor Dickinson. I thought this was great, but it was some time later when my Lord showed me humility. He indicated to me that I was in coaching not to win and promote Floyd Eby, but to have contacts and opportunities to promote the cause of Christ.

Praise God that He knows how to make a coach humble, by losing games. And that was to come.

My star guard, Dick has also found that there are more important things than winning state championships by shooting long shots. Dick has accepted the Lord and joined the Family of God due to the influence of his Christian daughters. Praise God for young people who are right with God.

* * *

My first night of basketball practice in my first year of coaching started a new trend in basketball. Not knowing the abilities of my personnel, I divided the players into two teams, gave the manager a whistle, and told them to go to it.

As I watched from the balcony, I noticed one player, Ron, staying down at the offensive bucket waiting for his teammates to throw him the ball. He did not go back on defense. I thought, "I will put that superstar in his place but quick."

I blew my whistle, and shouted at him.

THE BIRTH OF "RACE HORSE" BASKETBALL/31

"Who guarded your man last year, Ron?"

"Mac," he said.

"Who guarded Mac's man," I asked.

"Mac," Ron replied immediately.

"That's too bad, Ron, but Mac is not with us this year," I yelled sarcastically.

I blew my whistle and dismissed the entire squad.

Arriving home, I meditated on my situation. I needed Ron in the lineup as I already knew that he had led the team in scoring ever since he was a freshman. Ron, now a senior, would be most difficult to teach man to man defense. But how could my team play with a four man defense? It would have to be a zone of some sort.

I decided to use a four man box, and make Ron come back and chase the ball out front. This made the defense a box chaser or a one-two-two zone. This worked perfectly as Ron was a clever, energetic chaser. Every time he stole the ball, it was two points as no one could catch him. I also allowed him to chase the ball in the front court before he retreated. This added at least three buckets per game.

However, there were many leaks with this one man press. I sent Ron's half brother Rick down to help him. Wally came to the front court also, soon followed by Dean and Dick. Now, with all five players, zone pressing in the front court, we had blessed confusion to our advantage.

All teams thought we were pressing down court man to man, then dropping back into a zone. Our opponents were using man to man picks against our pressing zone, and we were "making hay" scoring almost at will on interceptions. In fact, when we threw a long pass out of bounds, many times it was a blessing in disguise as we immediately scored on an interception and fast break.

The turn-overs of our opponents, because of our chasing game, turned the game into "race-horse" basketball of chasing, running, shooting, and quick rebounding. Our starting five averaged only 5 feet, 8 inches, but our quickness and speed were paying off.

This "racehorse basketball" created a problem. We could

no longer come to a complete stop, put our feet together, and shoot the two handed set shot. So we started jumping in the air, throwing the ball at the basket, and shooting the one handed jump shot. People thought we were crazy. But it was the only way we could keep the fast tempo of the game moving, shoot over our taller opponents, and crash into the boards for some spirited rebounding.

* * *

Our opening game was at Napoleon, Michigan where my Uncle was the superintendent of schools, and my cousin played for the Napoleon basketball team.

At the end of the first quarter we were barely ahead by two points. I really felt that my starting five of Ron, Rick, Wally, Dean and Dick were not producing the results that I had expected. I substituted my second five, and told the starters to sit down on the bench and rest. I told them sarcastically that they looked tired.

Ron grabbed his jacket and moved down to the end of the bench. At the same time he mumbled loud enough for me to hear, "If I sit down on the bench and cool off, I won't be any good the rest of the night. I won't be able to hit a thing!"

I immediately jumped off the bench, and moved down and confronted Ron, "If you aren't any better player than you showed that first quarter, you are not near good enough to play on my team. I don't want to hear another word out of you, do you understand?"

"Yes Sir," he answered.

I put the starting five back in about midway of the second quarter, and we won the game handily, 44 to 30.

This was the last time I ever had any differences with my super star Ron. Ron was an excellent athlete and a wonderful guy. Ron was the most graceful, coordinated athlete I had been associated with. He was a well built, handsome young man about 5 feet 10 inches tall and about 165 pounds.

Ron had his hair parted in the middle, and was nearly always well-groomed. Because of his great coordination and gracefulness, he seemed to glide on the court and on the athletic fields. Opposing fans were always on Ron, because of his great ability. Ron would not show emotion.

He was sometimes considered a "show off" because of his great confidence in his own ability. He shot many hook shots in basketball when the hook shot was considered out of place and of no value. However, Ron's shooting percentage on all shots was fantastic.

Coach Eby with Ron Stover, one of his best athletes. He excelled in all high school sports.

Once he received the ball on the fast break, no one could stop him from scoring, even if he had to shoot a hook shot over the opponent's head. He scored over 400 points his senior year, which today would be comparable to 1,000 points.

Playing Brighton at home, Ron scored 30 points within a quarter and a half of playing time which is comparable to 70 points today. After the game the Brighton coach remarked, "I have never seen anything like it. If I were you, I would wrap that boy in several blankets, and keep him hot for the tournament."

We only lost one game during the regular season. Holt defeated us 28-26 in the second game.

In the district tournament at Leslie, we met Holt in the semi-finals. We were ahead one point with just a few seconds to go. Time was being kept by a little red clock at the bench. The fans and coaches could not really tell how much time was left. At the sounding of the gun, one of my players fouled a Holt player. Naturally, I argued.

"Ref, you know that gun sounded before you blew your whistle. The game is over and no free throw is allowed."

Smitty, the Holt coach disagreed. "No way, Ref, do you beat us out of that free throw. You know the gun and whistle sounded at the same time, and we have the right to a free throw."

As usual I lost the argument. The official agreed with Smitty and allowed the Holt player to shoot the free throw. He tied the game up 29 to 29, and we went into overtime.

With 46 seconds left in the overtime, we were behind 30 to 29, and we had a jump ball at midcourt.

The clock only stopped on fouls and time outs, so time was going to run out quickly. Harold, who substituted for Rick who had committed his fourth foul at the end of regulation time, tipped the jump ball, but Holt secured it.

We took it away from them with our press, and then a Holt player knocked it out of our hands. Everyone went after the ball but no one could get a handle on it. All this time the clock was moving. With only a few seconds left, Harold picked the ball off the floor at the keyhole and threw it at the basket. The ball bounded up and down on the rim, then settled on the top of the rim, and then finally fell through for the winning basket.

I jumped to my feet shouting and jumping with joy thinking that we had won the game. Before the gun went off a Holt guard took the ball out of bounds and threw it in to their center at mid-court who swished the basket clear from the center court.

I immediately sat down on the bench knowing that we had lost the game. But Dean took the ball out of bounds, and threw it to Wally at mid court --- who threw it through the basket just as the gun went off. Certainly, there wasn't much coaching strategy the last 30 seconds. But we won!

The next night on Saturday, we won the district basketball championship by defeating Okemos 38-30. This was the first district basketball championship that Williamston had ever won. The community and school were already excited, and talking day and night about going to the regionals.

The Albion regionals included three excellent teams: Nashville, Litchfield, and Jackson St. Marys. We drew Nashville for our first game. After winning the district, many of my coaching friends came to me with advice.

"Floyd, your style of basketball has been great for you in our league this year because of the small courts," they advised. "But on the big Albion court in the regionals, it will be suicide to stick to your 1-2-2 Zone, full court press, and fast break." "We suggest you go back to a tight man-to-man defense, dropping back as soon as the opposing team gets the ball."

I was convinced that I would have to change my system to have a chance to win in the regionals. We had just three nights of practice before our game with Nashville on Thursday night.

Monday night we started practicing a man-to-man defense, and we practiced slowing the game down. What a waste of time. In fifteen minutes I knew it was going to be impossible to change our system.

I stopped practice and gathered the squad on the floor at one end.

"Fellows, we are going to go with the same system of basketball in the regionals that has won for us all year," I said.

"The basket is the same size and height on all courts. We will position our zone according to the basket and free throw lane. We will not shift clear to the side on these large courts. Hustle, attitude, and conditioning has brought us this far and we can continue to win with it." I tried to say it convincingly.

On Thursday night we defeated a good Nashville team 35-21 which gave us the right to play Litchfield, the regional favorite, on Friday night. We wanted to be sure to have the same bench we had against Nashville. So we sent our manager, Frank over to the field house at noon with a bag of balls. We had him sit on the "lucky bench" all afternoon and up to game time.

We had our hands full with Litchfield. The large scoreboard was positioned so those who sat on the bench, could not see it. We would have to step out on the floor and look up to see the score and the time. I would then add to the score in my mind as we and Litchfield continued to score.

With only a minute to go, according to the score keeping of my mind, we were behind 33 to 32. Litchfield threw the ball out of bounds trying to work through our press. Dick took the ball out of bounds and threw it to Wally. Our team, instead of hurrying down the court as usual, and attempting to score, started stalling around with the ball. I hollered at them and told them to get going. We never --- but never --- stalled for the last shot when we were behind!

But the boys didn't pay any attention to me.

They just took their time and held onto the ball. As I knew would happen, the gun sounded ending the game before we even got a shot off and with us still holding the ball.

I was so mad, I decided right then and there that I wasn't going to give any of them their letters. What even made it worse was that our team seemed to be happy about losing.

Then the truth came out. The substitutes on the bench and I had made a mistake in computing the correct score. We had not been able to see the correct score on the scoreboard. During the last minute we had actually been ahead 33 to 32 instead of behind!

Our squad stayed in the Albion Hotel for the entire regional. Because we were over fifty miles from home, we could stay each night that we won, and the state athletic association would pay the expenses.

Most of the regional coaches were very strict with their players on what they ate and also on curfews. They insisted on their players going to their rooms right after the game. However, I allowed my players to eat as much as the state would pay for. After the game I would take my squad downtown bowling. Then to movies and other entertainment, until one or two o'clock in the morning, until some would ask to be able to go back to the rooms for rest.

Most of the coaches thought I was crazy and that we certainly were not going to win the regional championships. But I knew if I required my boys to be in early, that most of them would "horse" around in the rooms. Or they would go to sleep so early that they would get up too early in the morning. The players would then have all day to become tired before we played that night. When I took them back to the hotel at 2:00 a.m., they were so tired they would sleep until noon. We would then take a lot of time to have a good meal together, and then have a meeting. It wouldn't be long until the first game would be starting.

I knew it was vital to have unity among my players if we were going to go very far in the tournament. My policy was never to criticize any one of my players to anyone; just to the player himself. I insisted that my players never criticize me, but to come to me personally or bring up their "beef" in our meetings.

In one of our Albion meetings, I asked if anyone had anything to say to me before the squad. Wally spoke out. "Coach, in last night's game, I was standing wide open under the basket and Ron took a long shot instead of passing to me for an easy basket."

"Wally," I asked, "did Ron make the shot?"

"Yes, Coach," Wally answered.

"Do you realize Wally that if Ron had missed the shot, all you would have had to do was to get the rebound and put it in?   I never want to hear you criticize a teammate again," I said.   "Do you understand, Wally?"

"Yes, Sir." Wally answered softly.

I continued.   "I will decide who is shooting too much on this team, and who is not doing right. You just play ball and praise all your teammates."

Wally was one of the most outstanding athletes I ever coached. A tremendous football, basketball, and baseball player. A real competitor and team man, and a player that a coach never had trouble with. Wally also turned out to be an outstanding basketball coach in several high schools, and an oustanding husband, father, and Christian citizen.

We won the regional basketball championship on Saturday night by defeating Jackson St. Marys 32 to 27.   The community of Williamston was now going berserk thinking about us playing in the state quarter-finals. We added to the hysteria by defeating Wyandotte St. Patrick in the quarter finals 36-26 at Jackson.

The Wyandotte victory really put us in the "big time" by giving us the right to meet East Jordan in the Jenison Field House at Michigan State in the semi-finals. We were ahead of East Jordan at the end of the third quarter 29 to 13 before 13,000 screeching and screaming fans. Many of them were from Williamston which is located only 13 miles from Michigan State.

In fact the town was a "ghost" town that night as practically the entire community moved to Jenison Field House. Our 16 point lead at the end of the third quarter seemed plenty secure, as that is like a 35 point lead today. I pulled my five starters, and sent Wally, Dean, and Dick to the locker room to shower up.

I knew we were going to play the favorite, Keego Harbor,

the next night for the state championship. I thought it would be well for the three boys to shower, and not have to sit on the bench and cool off. I kept Ron and Rick on the bench with me in case one of my substitutes sprained an ankle or got some other injury. We only had ten players on the entire squad.

East Jordan started a comeback and we were outscored 13 to 1 the last quarter, winning the game 30 to 26. I really believe my coaching career would have ended right there if East Jordan had caught us and won the game. However, I was watching the scoreboard and the amount of time left. I never did put Ron and Rick back in. We had a six point lead when the gun went off. East Jordan had a long shot in the air at the time that swished through and closed the gap to four points.

The next night we won the state championship by defeating Keego Harbor 37 to 35. The secretary of the school board, Mr. Jones, came in the locker-room right after the victory and pulled me over to a corner. "Don't sign that next year's contract we gave you, we are going to give you a raise," he remarked!

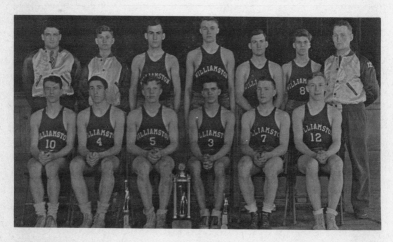

1940 Michigan State Class C Championship team - a team that changed basketball.

The next Monday, Leonard, our superintendent, called me in to his office. He congratulated me, and then said, "Coach, I want you to take this week off, and go down on the farm with your Dad, and relax." I did and it really helped me to get back to normal.

* * *

During the season the more experienced we became, the more effective our zone press and basic zone became. It became man-to-man defense while the opponent was in the individual players area. Then it became a smooth pattern of switching, and effective cover up.

We did everything possible to speed up the game --- sprinting to take the ball out of bounds; quick outlet passes; fast break as fast as we could run, sprinting back on defense, and no time outs. Our opponents in order to break our press had to fast break once they had broken through the first line of our defense. This helped to keep the tempo fast.

Because of the threat of our fast break, our opponents had to keep two guards back. On the defensive board, we always outnumbered the opponents four to three. When necessary, on a given signal, we could outnumber them five to three. Because of our basic zone and rebounding positions, we always had the same man in the same fast break lane each time. He became a specialist on what he had to do in his lane and area.

For example, our number two man always took the outlet pass over his left shoulder from a short circle path to the right. Each defensive rebounder had a number one and a number two option for his outlet pass. He could, many times, pass it out without looking, because he knew who and where his number one option was when he passed the ball.

Out of bounds in the back court, and after an opponent's basket, we would often throw a baseball pass the length of the court to catch our opponents napping and secure a cheap bucket. When they covered the long pass, this helped us open up the shorter fast break outlets.

THE BIRTH OF "RACE HORSE" BASKETBALL/41

As our opponents kept two guards back, our first three fast breakers would always beat the other three opponents down the floor. We would have three on two with our number four man coming down the lane as a fast trailer. We could hand off to him if the first three breakers were stopped.

We discarded the terminology of forwards, guards, and center. We numbered our players One-Two-Three-Four-Five, and made specialists out of them. This made it easier for substituting, out of bound plays, signals, jump balls, etc.

This also made it possible to confuse opponents when we were playing against a man-to-man defense. We could line up on jump balls in such a way that when their forwards were covering our fast break men, we could score several easy buckets before they could make adjustments.

When necessary, we used what we called our basic "Mike" defense, which was our box zone with our chaser man-to-man on their "hot shot." On rare occasions, we would use our number one and number two men on their two "hot shots," and use a triangle box zone defense.

Our basic offense was our fast break, full court press, and free lance patterns. We concentrated on even floor distribution with individual moves and drives against both man-to-man and zone defenses. We always emphasized our rebounding from pre-conceived rebounding positions for each player. Against the zone, we moved and drove on the first man, and then made a quick jump shot or pass off, with four men crashing the offensive board.

I am happy to see that most high schools, colleges, and pro's are now using many of these same ideas such as the one handed jump shot, fast break, zone full court press, basic one-two-two zone, and numbering system.

To play this system of basketball requires excellent physical condition. Also necessary is rigid discipline, training rules, desire, aggressiveness, players who are sold on the system, team work, harmony, and competitiors. We had all of this in my first team at Williamston in 1939-40 when we won the State Class C Championship, and also in the team at Coldwater in 1948-49 when we won the State Class B Championship.

I am proud of the players on these two teams and proud of the players on many other teams, not only for their athletic achievements, but because they all became outstanding citizens!

In deep humility, I wish to say that in no way do I wish to try to take any credit for the originating of any trends in basketball. I do praise God, however for using me in spite of my many inadequacies and mistakes to promote this wonderful game of basketball!

"I would hasten my escape from
the windy storm and tempest."
Psalm 55:8

3

ATTEMPTING TO ESCAPE

"If that dumb coach would have left the starting lineup alone, we would have won our 31st game in a row."

One of our school janitors angrily emphasized the reason for our loss.

"Who ever heard of such strategy, after winning thirty games in a row? To sit my boy on the bench, and start one of the substitutes --- it serves him right!" he continued.

The janitor was just one of our many interested fans who were now spoiled. After winning the state championship the previous year, and running our victory streak to thirty games, many of our wonderful and enthusiastic fans did not believe that we would ever lose another game.

In fact we had won the football championship again in the fall, and started out with a bang in basketball, winning one game after the other. Our fans were no longer betting on who would win the games --- but on how much we would beat them.

I started the second five in one game. I felt the starters

needed to be shook up. We were behind about six points at the start of the second quarter when I put my starters in. We then won the game handily by sixteen points.

Immediately after the game, one of our fans came down out of the bleachers, and confronted me on the floor. "Coach, how come you started the second five? You almost cost me a case of beer. I had bet we would win by 15 points. It's a good thing the starters came through!"

I turned and left for the locker-room.

Although we were in class C, I had scheduled two of the better class B schools in the state to give us tougher competition to ready us for the tournaments.

After winning 30 in a row, we played class B power-house Mt. Pleasant in the Central Michigan College fieldhouse. It was a big deal for us as Mt. Pleasant College was playing another college in the preliminary, and we were playing Mt. Pleasant High School in the second game. My players and I wanted to win it in the worst way.

During the week of practice, I tried to find an even stronger starting five. Irwin, a substitute guard, had been improving rapidly. So I started him in Glen's place. We lost the game by two points, decided right at the end of the game. Our fans could not understand it. After all, Williamston was not supposed to lose any games, and of course Glen's father let his feelings be known.

However, I stuck to the same lineup the next week. We pulled a real upset by trouncing class B powerhouse East Lansing on their own court. This eased the tension just a little.

We went on winning the rest of our games and the league championship. We were favorites to win the district tournament championship, but were upset by our old nemises, Holt. That ended the season.

Our season's record of 15 wins and two losses was just not good enough. Comments were heard and every teacher on the staff received a raise except me. The Lord sure knows how to keep a coach humble. I praise God, because I could have been given a cut!

I knew at the end of this year I was going to lose, by graduation, nearly all of my good athletes from the football, basketball, and baseball teams. In basketball, I was losing four starters with only Dick back at guard. I thought it might be a good time to leave.

I received a letter from the Superintendent of schools of Coldwater, Michigan. He stated that the head football coaching job at Coldwater was open, and he would like to have me apply.

"Great," I thought. "This will allow me to escape the beatings next year that the league coaches had planned for me." I applied by letter, and then checked out the town of Coldwater. It seemed to be a good spot to move to even though the indoor facilities were not too good. The teams had been down for a couple of years, and a coach would have an opportunity to build up the athletic program.

Coldwater High School had 72 applicants for the head football job. Smith, former captain of the Michigan State football team; Amers from Ionia; Jones from Illinois; and I were still on the list after much screening had taken place. We four were invited to come to Coldwater the same night and meet with the board, principal, and superintendent. We were asked to come in one at a time and be interviewed by the board and administration while the other three waited outdoors.

I wanted the job so badly, I was really worried about "goofing up" on the interview. When my turn came, I felt like the score was tied, and we were in overtime and the opposing team had the ball. I was asked some routine questions.

Then one of the men who was smoking a big cigar asked me about my training rules. Even though I felt my answers were going to hurt my chances, I gave them my exact training rules, as well as my other rules on conduct and discipline.

My interview was over and I went back outdoors with the other applicants. After the last fellow had been interviewed, we four remained outdoors for three hours as the Board was making its decision.

"There must be some real disagreements in that decision making meeting," commented Amers from Ionia. "We sure know that whoever they choose, it will be a close vote. The winner will still have some opponents on the Board." All of us agreed.

At midnight the superintendent came out to talk with us. "Gentlemen, I am real sorry that you had to wait so long, but the Board wanted to be sure to hire the right man. I am happy to inform you that the Board has unanimously accepted Mr. Jones from Illinois as that man.

"I wish to thank you other three for your time and consideration. You can all leave, except Mr. Jones. The Board would like to talk to him."

Amers and Smith were somewhat put out for the way the interviews were made and the length of time we had had to wait for the decision. I stepped up to the superintendent and shook his hand. "I wish to thank you and the board kindly for your consideration. I wish Mr. Jones a fine coaching career at Coldwater."

Admittedly I was disappointed. My wife and a couple of friends had been waiting in the car for hours. Now I would have to go back to Williamston and absorb those beatings the next year and try to build another winner. I didn't know it then, but this turn down was a blessing in disguise.

* * *

The next fall our football field was in a mess. Before we could start practice, I had to borrow a saw. The players and I cut up and hauled off a big tree the storms had blown down. I borrowed a large farm mower and farm rake to cut and rake the weeds. I raked them off by pulling this machinery with my old car. We had a mediocre season winning half our games.

Basketball practice started, and prospects appeared terrible. The second week of practice I invited the previous year seniors back to scrimmage us. They beat us 76 to 13. I really felt sorry for myself, and more and more I wished I had received that Coldwater job.

Our opening game was at Napoleon. I drove the school bus on this long trip. Our two cheerleaders rode on the bus. I made them sit in the seat directly back of me, the driver. Sitting right back of the cheerleaders were two of the players. One of them, Toby, chatted and kidded with the girls on the entire trip.

Instead of telling him to shut up, I boiled inside all the way there. I thought how stupid it was for Toby to be enjoying himself when we had an important game coming up. I thought to myself, "Toby better play a good game tonight or I will let him have it."

At half time we were behind six points. I guess I was as bad as our fans. I was spoiled also. I felt sorry for myself for the bad season coming up. During the half time locker room session, I really took Toby apart.

"You can really see what is wrong with this team, by the way certain players act. Toby is so concerned about us having a winning season, that he spent the entire bus ride down here gabbing with the cheerleaders. No wonder his play stinks. His heart isn't in it. All he wants to do is to play lovey-dovey with the girls."

The more I chewed him out, the madder I became. I worked myself up to such a frenzy, that I picked up a steel chair and threw it at him. Toby had no trouble ducking it as it slammed into the concrete locker room wall. There wasn't much said after that as we trooped out onto the floor to play the second half.

Everything seemed to go wrong. Dick lost his glasses on the floor, and the kids stopped to pick them up before someone stepped on them. Even a couple of Napoleon players started to pick them up. The basketball rolled over to the side. My cousin, Don, who played for Napoleon, nonchalantly picked up the ball and dribbled it and shot a basket. The crazy official counted the basket instead of calling an emergency timeout. This upset me even more. I hollered some unkind words in his direction.

Later in the game, a Napoleon player shot from the corner. It hit on the ledge and bounded on across. Dick, positioning himself under the basket, touched the net as the ball bounced clear to the other side of the court. The basketball net was twice as long as the average net, even so the incompetent official awarded Napoleon a basket because Dick touched the net.

We lost the game 27 to 25 with my cousin scoring 12 out of the 27 Napoleon points. This made things even worse. This annual Napoleon opener had become a family feud between my family and my Uncle's family, the superintendent of Napoleon.

We lost another game, and then our team really began to jell. The more we won, the stronger we developed. We won the league championship, and then the district championship which once against put us into the regionals at Albion.

We won the first game in the regional, and then defeated Jackson St. Marys 25 to 23 in the semi-finals. Our regional opponent in the finals was the same Napoleon team that beat us in the opening game with my cousin doing most of the damage.

I took my substitute guard, Ken, aside. "Ken, I am going to start you in the Napoleon game in place of Dick. You will be on the side where Napoleon's forward, Don, will be driving the basket. Don almost always fakes right and then drives left around the horn and to the basket. The first four times he tries this drive, I want you to commit the four fouls you are allowed. Don't you dare let him get to that basket. When you are ejected with four fouls, your job for the night will have been completed."

Ken did just as he was told. The Napoleon star forward, Don, picked himself up off the floor the first four times he tried to drive the basket, and Ken left the game. Don was so "shook up" that he missed every free throw. Dick had an easy time with him the rest of the game, and we held Don to no points. We won the game 36 to 23, winning the regional championship for the second time in three years.

The next Thursday we played Tecumseh in the state

quarter finals. Smitty, our tall center who was our top rebounder, and our second top scorer, became sick with strep throat. He could not play. We lost to Tecumseh 35 to 33 ending our season with 20 wins and 3 losses.

The team that season had taught me much. I found that I did not need to feel sorry for myself. I now realize that real hustle, desire, and dedication can always make up for lack of ability. This team because of these characteristics improved more in one season that any other I ever coached.

Most of all, this team taught me that I didn't need to try and escape from seemingly bad situations. I could face my situations, trust in the Lord, and work things out. I didn't have to run from "the windy storm and tempest."

* * *

In the fourth year of my coaching at Williamston, we had an even-steven season in football. Once again we had an excellent season in basketball losing only three games. However, we had a real problem with the tournaments. That season, 1943-44, was the year of war gas rationing.

I was on the state tournament committee for the state athletic association. This committee was made up of superintendents, principals, state officials, and two coaches including myself. The committee had to make the decision of whether to go on with the state basketball tourney or call it off because of the critical gas shortage. I felt that we had the team that could go all the way that year and win the state championship. Naturally, I plugged to keep the tournament as usual.

Gentlemen, I believe our basketball program should carry on," I said. "We know that the physical condition of our youth is important to our national welfare. Attendance is not the issue. I will see that my team gets there if we have to use horses. As far as I know, there is only one other state that is calling off their basketball tournaments. All other states are going ahead as normal."

However, my pleas fell on mostly deaf ears. The

superintendents, principals, and state officials weren't likely to listen to a coach who was prejudiced because he had a good team. I guessed I really was somewhat selfish, but I wanted my team to win another state Championship.

As sort of a compromise, the committee settled on area tournaments, where people would not have to travel very far to watch their favorites play. I was in a good position, being on the committee, to set up a powerful class C area tournament in Lansing which was the largest in the state. This tourney had several of the highest rated C teams in the state including Williamston.

We won four games in a row, and won the Area Championship. I rationalized that it was like winning the state championship because it was the largest and most powerful area tourney. I expect there were several other area class C champions that felt the same way.

* * *

After the basketball season and unknown to me, the Coldwater School superintendent visited our community. Among others, he visited with our local druggist, one of my best friends. He didn't tell our druggist who he was but just said, "I am a stranger in town; what kind of athletic program and coach do you have?" The druggist built our program and coach up to this stranger.

The superintendent remarked, "I am the superintendent of schools in Coldwater, Michigan, and we are thinking about hiring your coach." The druggist replied, "Everything I told you is an exaggerated lie."

Not knowing that I was being investigated, I was really surprised when I received a letter from the Coldwater superintendent with the following information. "Our football job is once again open, and we have 82 applicants for the position. However, with this letter we are offering you a contract to hire you to fill this position. Would you please contact me soon. We will make arrangements to officially have you sign the contract."

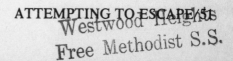

I wrote back to the Superintendent and thanked him and the board for their consideration, but I was no longer interested. I really wasn't trying to be cagey. I had made up my mind that Williamston had been so good to me that I wanted it to be my home for life. I also had found that losing star players by graduations didn't have to always mean failure.

Once Coldwater found I wasn't interested, they really were stimulated to secure my services. The superintendent wrote again and then called me on the phone urging me to at least come and talk with him. I agreed that in three weeks I would stop in and see him. I was scheduled to pass through Coldwater on my way home for a visit.

In the office of the superintendent, he asked, "Why are you not interested in our job any more?"

"Sir," I answered, "two years ago, you and the board did not want me. I am the same man, teacher, and coach that I was then. Therefore, if I was not good for this school and community two years ago, I will not be any good for you now."

"Mr Eby, I guess I am going to have to tell you something that I didn't want to. If you remember, we had a long session that night as you four applicants waited. Everyone was in favor of hiring you including the principal and I, and all board members except the president of the board. We wanted to make it unanimous, but he insisted on hiring Mr. Jones. During your long wait we were arguing with him to change his mind. He kept insisting on Mr. Jones so we all gave in, and went along with him. He is no longer on the board, and we are now in total agreement that you are the man we need.

"Now, what other objections do you having in signing our contract offer?" he inquired.

"Well," I answered, "your job is a head football coaching job. I am not ready or willing to give up basketball and baseball coaching."

He replied, "We are willing to make you athletic director and you can head coach any sport you desire. We will hire assistants to help you."

Well, that just about did it.

"I have to admit, sir, that your offer is now real attractive," I said. "but because of the War and draft, I don't believe I will be around much longer."

"We are willing to take that chance," he responded, "and we will assure you of your job on your return from the service."

I promised him I would go home and think it over and let him know in two weeks. When I arrived back in Williamston, I also had an offer from Lansing Everett.

When Williamston found out about the two other offers, they made my position at Williamston even more attractive in added pay and responsibilities. Salary offered at Williamston topped both Lansing Everett and Coldwater, with Coldwater the lowest. However, I knew that Williamston was offering to pay me more than they should just to keep me. I knew this would present problems with the other teachers in the future.

Within two weeks, I made the most difficult decision of my young coaching career. I decided to leave all of my wonderful friends in Williamston and move to Coldwater. I could hardly take it when I said goodbye. I almost bawled!

"Eby, how could you have ever been so interested in escaping from this wonderful community two years ago, just because you lost some good boys by graduation?" I asked myself.

"I was a stranger,
and ye took me in"
Matthew 25:35

4

THE STRANGER IN TOWN

"Hey, Jack, can't you get it in your head?" I shouted.

I had just started my football coaching job at Coldwater High School. I knew very few boys by name. They were all new to me. This was the second week of football practice. We were scrimmaging. I was trying to show my halfback, Jack, how to run the left end.

"There are two ways to do it," I said. "First, as we snap the ball to you through the quarterback's legs, you will take your first two steps up toward the tackle hole. As the defensive end sucks in, the wingback will hit him. Then you will pivot on your right foot and cut off the tail of the wingback and head for the sidelines and daylight. You understand, Jack?"

"Yeh, Coach," Jack confirmed.

I continued, "Now, Jack, the other way is to take your first two steps parallel to the line of scrimmage. The defensive end will start to cover you wide, our left guard will pull and block him out. You will pivot up field on your left foot, cut off the tail of our blocking guard, and when through the hole, head for the sidelines and daylight."

"Yeh, Coach," Jack agreed.

However, Jack just didn't seem to be able to get it right, so I told him to watch me.

Being the coach, I did not have a football uniform on; just football cleats, baseball pants, whistle, and T shirt. Huddling up, I called my play number, and received the ball. I took the first two steps up toward the tackle hole, the defensive end sucked in, our wingback hit him from the outside. I pivoted on my right foot, and cut off the tail of our wingback and headed for the sidelines, and daylight.

I was speeding along carrying the pigskin for about thirty yards, when something hit me right at the knees like a ton of bricks.

As I was going down, I thought to myself, "I want to know that boy's name. Anyone who can hit like that, I can use."

As I settled to the ground with this guy on top of me, I could hardly wait to learn his name. A 195 pounder got up off me. I jumped to my feet and said, "What is your name, son?"

"Carl," he said, grinning sheepishly.

I was thinking, I hope he is only a junior and not a senior so I can use him for two years. I said, "What grade are you in, Carl?"

"Sixth," he answered.

Here Carl was, a sixth grader, down practicing with the varsity. I had to wait patiently for three years before I could use him four straight years as my varsity fullback.

By then he had grown up, still five feet, eight inches tall, but now 245 pounds. He was incredibly hard to bring down. I praise God for Carl because he not only became my fullback, but also became my brother in Christ. He and his wife also have two fine Christian athletes of their own.

* * *

I had moved to Coldwater in August. My co-worker, Bert, had been a coach at Coldwater for many years, and is a wonderful man. He was a great help in getting me oriented with the community, schools, and the players. I soon learned from Bert that we had not only lost several good players by graduation, but six other regulars had either moved or had gone in to the service. Losing their other head coach had not helped the situation.

In the evenings, I would go to Waterworks Park to watch the softball games, and to get acquainted with the people and the high school athletes. I didn't let anyone know that I was the new coach in town. Everyone thought I was a stranger, visiting for the summer.

I made friends with many people and athletes without telling my name and who I was. They gave me much information about the school, and all about the athletes coming back. Many of the athletes talked with me personally about the teams. I recognized many of their names because Bert had given me an eligibility list and told me about many different boys.

As I talked with many of these athletes, I found out many things about them. They thought they were visiting with a stranger. Many were smoking and cursing, and telling me about the wild parties they were having that summer. Being a strict disciplinarian on training rules, I was already discouraged with what I found out. At Williamston we had training rules the year around, including the summer.

Just before school opened, I called a meeting of all candidates for the football squad. Naturally, I was the first one there, opening up one of our classrooms for the meeting. As the boys trooped through the door, and took one long look at me, they suddenly realized that the visiting stranger in town was actually the new coach. I am sure that many were tempted to turn and leave, as they realized that the new coach already knew about their personal habits.

I gave each one a cordial greeting as they came through the door. I understood that between coaching regimes it was a natural reaction for athletes to sow their wild oats.

I called the meeting to order.

"I am your new coach, Coach Floyd Eby," I said.

"I have met many of you at Waterworks Park this summer. I know much more about each one of you than you know about me. However, I am not interested in the past, but only the present and your future. I am holding you responsible for your actions and conduct from this meeting on. The rules I set up tonight for all members of the Coldwater High School Football Team, will be strictly enforced. Anyone breaking these rules will be eliminating themselves from the football squad.

"You see, you kick yourself off the squad when you break the rules. I don't do it, you do. I am only interested in two accomplishments: one, to train football players to become outstanding citizens of this school and community. Second, to train football players so Coldwater High School can have a winning football team, and one that will properly represent this school and community in all ways."

* * *

We were having a mediocre season. A twelve-car caravan traveled from Williamston to Coldwater to watch us play Hillsdale. It was a great night for us as we swamped Hillsdale. It was so good to see many of my friends from Williamston, and to win decisively on the night they came.

Coldwater had not beaten Albion in football for many, many years. Albion had another excellent team this year. I planned for weeks to beat Albion. I knew if we pulled off this upset, it would be a very successful season.

We were hurting with some injuries so I had brought two freshmen, Ron and John, up to the varsity. I planned to use both of them in this potential upset at Albion. Ron was a very definite part of our plans to upset Albion.

As I came to our home locker room to load the equipment and players in cars to make the trip to Albion, I went to my office. On my desk was a short note from my principal, Mr. Smith.

"Dear Coach, Ron was staying in study hall after school making up time for being tardy. He walked out early, and gave the study hall teacher some lip. Please do not take him to Albion tonight."

I really was uptight. The squad and coaching staff had worked so hard to attempt to pull off this big upset. Now our chances were going down the drain because of a "smart alec" freshman. Besides, this went against my theory of punishment. I believed this action by our principal was punishing the entire squad since it was too late to change our personnel and strategy. I believe that a boy like Ron should be punished by missing the next week's game. Then the coach and squad would have the opportunity to replace him.

I tried to call Mr. Smith, but didn't find anyone at home. Being new, I wanted to be sure I cooperated with my principal who was a fine gentleman. However, since I couldn't reach him, I made my own decision, and took Ron with us.

As I called off the starting lineup in the locker-room, I took Ron apart.

"Fellows, we have a freshman on this varsity squad who has done his best to keep us from pulling this upset." I related to the squad what Ron had done.

Then I shouted directly at him, "Ron, I would never have brought you up to the Varsity, if I realized what a bum you are. Anyone who would try to destroy several weeks of his teammates hard work, by shooting off his lip to a teacher, and acting like he owns the school by walking out early, has to be one of the great imposters of all times.

"Ron, there is no room for boys like you on this varsity squad. I am going to play you tonight for the sake of your teammates. As far as you are concerned, you could rot in that study hall. Next week, you will not be allowed to practice or to play in the game. If you ever pull another trick like this, you will be through forever. Do you understand?

Ron nodded and kept his head down.

We used two special plays that night, time after time. A trapblock run off of tackle and a short pass to our left end.

We trounced Albion by two touchdowns. It was a great night as Albion didn't know what hit them. I believe the incident of Ron's misbehavior really fired our entire squad up.

As soon as I arrived home, I contacted Mr. Smith and explained the situation and what I had done. He was gracious to me, and agreed that my way was a good way to handle Ron. I praised God for administrators you can talk with.

Ron straightened out. He became an all-star athlete in football, basketball, and baseball for four years at Coldwater High, including being the league leader in scoring in basketball his senior year.

* * *

I was also the physical training instructor at Coldwater High School. Due to emphasis from the Pentagon at Washington, D.C., much pressure was placed on the secondary schools to get the boys in top physical shape for induction into the armed forces.

I had organized a complete program. All high school boys, except those excused by a doctor, were required to take the course five days each week including the athletes. The course was tough. Besides the games used for body building and recreation, the course also consisted of callisthenics, obstacle courses, cross country running, and special physical tests.

Each Monday, in good or bad weather, we would start each class period off with a 2½ mile cross country run. I would line the class up in the gym, take attendance, and then shoo them out through the door.

I didn't run the course myself because I had seven classes in a row. I followed them with my bicycle to see that they didn't cheat by short cutting the course.

"OK guys, get going. Let's build up that endurance," I said one morning, as I shooed them out the door. As usual I waited a couple of minutes, then went out to get my bicycle to follow them. Someone had let the air out of my rear tire, to prevent me from following.

I immediately borrowed another bike, and soon caught up with them. It was a year later before I found out that it was the mayor of the school, Doug, always a very resourceful person, who had let the air out of my tire.

All of my main athletes were grouped in the last period of the day. Immediately after physical education class, the athletes would get dressed for practice. On the day of the game, I excused them from participating in the course activities. They would sit on the sidelines. My athletes in the seventh hour class were constantly kidding me about running the cross country course with them.

I knew they really wanted to show me up. However, I felt peddling my bicycle 2½ miles every class period seven times during the day was enough exercise for me. But one day I gave in to them.

"Come on coach, show us what you can do," they kidded.

"OK, fellows, just this once I will run it with you," I answered. I had already ridden my bike six times over the course that day.

We took off together. Naturally the kids ran extra fast to show me up, and they soon left me behind. I was already tired from 15 miles of bike riding that day, and I wondered if I could run the whole course. I realized that I had to or I would never hear the last of it.

By the time I reached Morgan's store, I thought I was going to die. When I chugged into the fairgrounds, I knew I was going to die, but I just had to go on. I had now passed some of my athletes who had started out too fast.

While loping through the fair grounds, I received my second wind and actually felt much better. I was then determined to pass as many as I could even though I was pushing myself more than I should. I arrived at the gym in 3rd place, but in such condition that I could hardly pull myself up the locker room stairs with the use of the railing. That was the last time I ever ran the course.

* * *

Football season ended, and we started my first basketball season at Coldwater. The former basketball coach had used a slow, deliberate, pattern style of play. It was a great adjustment for the kids to change to "race horse" basketball.

It included the full court zone press, one handed jump shooting, constant running, and aggressive body contact. Also a free lance style of play including diving for loose balls, and crashing rebounding. After last year's style of play, this new brand of basketball seemed real wild to the players. However, they seemed to like it, and worked hard to overcome their shortcomings.

We opened the season with Three Rivers in our small gym. We lost by five points. The official, opposing coach, players, and all of the fans, could not believe what they were seeing. At this time we were real rough and uncouth in trying to play this race horse basketball. The official had more than he could handle. He came over to me at the first timeout.

"What is this anyway, the Eby blitz? Man, you can't continue this very long."

The fans were reacting strongly, by screeching and screaming. Our fans loved it and the Three Rivers fans hated it. News traveled rapidly all over the league, and all schools except Coldwater immediately hired two officials for all Coldwater games.

We defeated Albion and the Albion paper reported: "Albion's fair to middling team got its first taste of Coldwater's body checking, race horse team Friday night --- and did not like it . . . But the shock that such a style of ball could be perpetrated left the Albion boys much in the condition of an inland lake swimmer suddenly jumping into the waters of Lake Superior . . . . Next time, it will be different --- perhaps."

"Could they do it with two officials? After suffering defeat at Coldwater's hands, every team is going to ask if it could happen with two officials on the floor (as the Twin Valley still sticks to the one official system, in contrast with most other state leagues, big or small.)...."

Last Tuesday night, Coldwater won a two-official game

from Three Rivers 27 to 22 after having 30 fouls called upon them and five of their players sent to the showers ... Main reason was that Three Rivers, after having won in December at Coldwater, was so shocked at the spectacle that it 'lost its fight somewhere along the way' and only made 11 out of 31 free throws ... As the Three Rivers Commercial reported the foray, it was: 'From late in the first quarter onward, it was slam-bang, slip and slide ... It isn't basketball, but it's effective -- for Coldwater ... The Cardinals' wild style of play caught up Coach Francis Pellegrom's chargers in the heat of the thing and the Cats unlearned almost what they'd learned about the game of basketball.'

"Probably the best formula to beat such a team is to let bedlam reign in all scrimmages for a week before hand, use football shoulder pads on the more shy players, practice free throws diligently and hire a second official ... If that does not work, there is nothing to be done but grin and bear it ... For, as we said in our original report of last Friday's game, there is nothing vicious or dirty about Coldwater's play."

During the season there were many newspaper articles criticizing our unusual style of play. We continued to improve, and ended the season winning a little over half our games. This was a very successful season as far as our fans were concerned, as last year's team had won only one game, and that by the score of 14-13. Our fans were excited about all the action and controversy about our style of play.

Our team was rough and tough. All of our basketball players were also football players. I believe that football gave us the toughness to rebound, and aggressiveness to full court press and race horse, and the stamina and competitiveness to endure and survive.

I told my guard, Bill, that if he was going to foul a man who was going in for a dog shot, to make sure he didn't make the shot. Sometimes I regretted telling Bill this as he would mow down the man making sure the basket would not go in. Later on, Bill became an all-star football end in a large College, and also an outstanding high school coach. The other guard, also named Bill, became a great football player, and he fouled out of nearly every game --- usually early.

Smitty was one of the best and smoothest players we had, and was just terrific in every practice. However, Smitty was so nervous before each game that as I called off the starting lineup including Smitty, he would become sick and start vomiting. Every game, the same thing would happen. No way was I able to use Smitty even though he was one of the best players in the league during practice. However, he stayed out and kept trying.

* * *

When I moved from Williamston to Coldwater, I told my draft board at Mason that for June, July, and August, I would be working for my father on his farm. If my call came up, they could reach me at his address. However, if my call came up after September 1, I would be at the Coldwater High School where I had taken a new job.

I received no notice from them during the summer. So when I moved to Coldwater in September, I notified them and told them I was moving from the farm to Coldwater. The draft board misunderstood my intentions. They assumed I had gone to work on the farm to get out of going to war, and now felt safe and was leaving the farm for a better job.

They immediately notified me to get back on the farm or they would change my classification to 1A. I wrote back and explained that I had never intended to attempt to delay my departure to the service. No way was I going back on the farm as I had signed a teaching and coaching contract at Coldwater High School. The draft board wrote back and classified me 1A. I wrote back and demanded my immediate release so I could enlist.

I set up an appointment with the Naval and Air Force recruiters in Detroit. Several months later I was called to Detroit for tests. I spent several days applying for a commission in the United States Navy, and also applying to enter the U.S. Army Air Force. I thought if I didn't receive my officers commission in the Navy, I would go to the Air Force.

Going back to my teaching and coaching job at Coldwater, I waited for news of my acceptance or rejection in one or both of these services. I heard first from the Air Force who sent orders for me to report to the commanding officer of an Air Force base in Illinois. I really didn't want to go into the Air Force unless I was unable to obtain a commission in the Navy. I was the maximum age of 26 to start training as an Air Force pilot. I felt if I washed out I would end up in the Infantry.

I stalled, hoping and praying I would hear from the Navy, before the Air Force came looking for me. I now knew if I didn't receive my commission through this stalling, I would be in serious difficulty with the Air Force for reporting so late. Every day as the mail came I would be uptight.

Finally the long awaited letter from the Navy came. Fortunately, they had commissioned me an Ensign in the U.S. Navy. I was not scheduled to report until April, which allowed me to coach football and basketball, and only miss the baseball season. I also had time to settle my plans for my job and my family.

Everyone was gracious about inviting me back after the war. I was promised my job back by the administration and the school board. I didn't really want to leave, but I knew I did not want to shirk my responsibility to my Country which has done so much for me.

After serving two years overseas in the United States Navy during the war, I returned to Coldwater High School to continue my coaching and teaching career. God is so good!

5

THE BIRTH OF SPLIT T FOOTBALL
AND THE OPEN HUDDLE

"Coach, where are they going to crown the Queen at halftime?" the photographer asked, as he knelt directly in front of me, blocking my vision to the game action.

"Get out of my way you sap," I shouted at him. "I don't care where or when you crown her, just get out of my way --- now!"

The photographer got out of there but quick.

I was kneeling on one knee watching the Sturgis football team driving toward our goal in the most important game of the season. Sturgis was making three to five yards a crack as they relentlessly powered toward our goal line. They had already reached the fourteen yard line with ninety seconds to go in the half. We were only ahead 6 to 0, and it was imperative that we stop them from scoring before the half. Sturgis had cut our defense to ribbons in this 75 yard drive.

On each play I was sending in a substitute with orders to move a line backer, a tackle or a guard, trying to stop the trapblocks over my guards and the powerful slashes off tackle. I was having my problems. The kids were excited too. Most of the time they didn't get the messages in time to the right defensive player, or they would misunderstand.

"For Pete's sake, Callahan, tell that McCurley to line up on the outside shoulder of our defensive tackle on the strong side," I told Callahan to tell McCurley. "They're killing us outside that tackle."

Callahan sprinted to the field, and the photographer knelt in front of me just as Sturgis ran the next play. I couldn't see a thing and didn't know if Sturgis made any ground or whether they went fourteen yards for the score. Fortunately, we stopped Sturgis on the eight yard line and stalled out the half, and maintained our six point lead.

I still don't know if that photographer got a picture of the crowning of our Homecoming Queen.

Sturgis all-conference fullback, Patton, was one of the most powerful runners in the entire state. McCurley, my middle line backer, weighed only 145 pounds, compared to Patton's 200 pounds. Mac was a great backer-upper. Because of his lack of size and the fact he hit so low and hard, he was always getting hurt --- not to the extent that he couldn't play effectively, but he seemed always to be limping.

One of the Sturgis coaches had warned me all season long about the approaching catastrophe for Mac.

"Coach," the Sturgis coach had told me again and again "Patton will hurt McCurley seriously, when we play you! You had better keep Mac on the bench during our game! If Mac hits Patton head on like he does these smaller backs, you will have to take Mac to the hospital or the morgue," the Sturgis coach continued. "I really dread to think what might happen."

"Baloney," I said. "Mac is tougher than you think. And you are over-rating Patton."

I really was trying to reassure myself that the Sturgis coach was wrong. I had visions about Mac hitting Patton, and Mac having to be carried off the field.

In the third quarter of the game with Sturgis, Patton

carried the ball right up the middle on a guard trap play. There was a big hole but Mac came rushing through the hole right at Patton, and met him head on. It sounded like a couple of trucks meeting each other.

Both Mac and Patton went down hard, and laid there with Mac on top. "Oh," I thought, "this is the time I will need a stretcher for Mac." I rushed out to the pile. Just as I arrived, Mac struggled to his feet and shook his head a couple of times.

"Are you all right, Mac?" I asked.

"Yeh," he answered. "Please help Patton off the field."

Patton was carried off the field, and he never played again that night. We won the game 12 to 6. Mac was a bit hard to live with the rest of the season, but he continued to hit --- low and hard.

* * *

The next season during the first week of practice I found out what I already knew. Our backs did not have the speed to run the ends. I knew our running game would suffer as all the other coaches in our league knew the same thing about our backs. The opposing coaches would close in with their defense and make it impossible to run anywhere.

No way could we keep them honest. We, like all other teams at the time, had a close knit lineup. The center, guards, and tackles, lined up right next to each other, and the ends probably split one yard from the tackles in our offensive line play.

There was no way that I was going to be able to have any fast backs. I had to come up with something or suffer through a miserable season. What could it be? The single wing couldn't help me. My interference was also slow and the defense could sift through the blockers before we could skirt the ends.

Suddenly, I thought, "Why don't I move my wingback out to a flanker and split my offensive ends way out on both sides. This should force the defensive ends, the outside line backers, or the defensive halfbacks to go out to cover. Someone also would have to cover my flanker. Then I decided to move both offensive tackles for several yards splits, then the guards were also split.

It sure looked crazy with the offensive line spread across the field with the center alone in the middle with only the guards and three backs anywhere near him. Of course I didn't have any idea how our opponents would react defensively to this. However, I was hoping they would split their defense with our split offensive line."

You can't imagine how surprised our opponents were in that first game.

When we came out of the huddle, all our players sprinted to far away places to set for the snap. We snapped the ball in a hurry and started running wide to our right. It was like running through a herd of cattle. Everyone was running all over the place. After we had made a 12 yard gain, Three Rivers called time out.

Before the game I told my team: "After our very first play, Three Rivers will call time out. After the time out, and we call our second play, go to our set places. Then hold for about ten seconds, and give them time to arrange their defense. I just know they will shift men out with each one of our offensive men. Then call our regular game plan which is to run up the center, off the guards, and off tackle."

The holes we had already made were huge. All our offensive players had to do was to brush and screen block, and we would go for 5 to 10 yards every play. Even though Three Rivers made many adjustments, we piled up tremendous yardage. For two straight years we ran wild with our slow backs. We varied the distance of the split from play to play.

The birth of Split T Football was assured as many other teams started doing the same. After two years we still had our problems with our slow backs. The opposing coaches realized that there was no way we could run the end. They closed in tight and kept us somewhat under control, but the Split-T was here to stay.

* * *

Up to this time no football teams had ever used a defensive huddle. Certain defensive players would just holler certain instructions to their team mates, wherever they were placed.

I thought to myself, why wouldn't it be smart to huddle on defense at the same time our opponents were huddling on offense? When they broke out of their huddle, we could then break out of ours.

In this way, the offensive players would not see our locations as they came up to the line. Our defensive players would all know the plans of all eleven of our team mates on this particular play, and could even discuss special needs. We now could use a quarterback (signal caller) on defense.

The defensive huddle caught on quickly with other teams, and soon all teams were using their variation of the defensive huddle.

At the time, we were using the commonly used circle offensive huddle on offense. Our quarterback, Gene, was calling all of the plays. Theoretically, the only others players allowed to say anything in the huddle were the captain and center. All other players were to relay their thoughts to one of these three before they gathered into the circle huddle. Of course a messenger sent in by the coach superseded all other calls.

At half-time I pulled my quarterback, Gene, off to a corner of the dressing room by myself.

"For crying out loud, Gene," I exclaimed. "What's the matter with you tonight? Your play-calling stinks. I can't seem to get anything across to you with messengers. I want to know what's going on in that huddle, anyhow?"

"Honest coach," he answered, "I can't hear a thing in that huddle. Everyone is jabbering at me all at once. I can't even think with all that hullaboo going on. I can't even hear the messages you send in. It has been steadily getting worse for the last two weeks."

"Why didn't you let me know what was going on?" I demanded.

THE BIRTH OF SPLIT T FOOTBALL/69

"Well, coach," he mumbled softly, "I just didn't want to say anything."

I demanded silence in the huddle for the next half, but I knew this would only be temporary as we played other games.

I decided that I would have to come up with something that would permanently solve this problem. I had studied on it all weekend, and during practice the following week I really felt I had the answer.

For our basic offensive formation, we were using a split-T with a wingback or flanker on either side. Naturally, the quarterback was directly back of center to take the snap, and the two set backs, fullback and a halfback, 3 yards back of the quarterback.

My new idea to solve my talking problem in our offensive huddle was to devise an offensive huddle which I called the "open huddle."

I had my center go back eight yards from the line of scrimmage, and line up facing the ball. The right guard and tackle, and the left guard and tackle were in the same line on their respective sides. I required this front line to bend over with their hands on their knees and look straight ahead.

In the back line of the two line huddle, I had the fullback position himself directly back of the center. The right halfback and right end, and the left halfback and left end, were on their respective sides of the fullback. The back line was standing straight up and looking dead ahead.

The quarterback would step to the huddle facing the center and the rest of the huddle with his back to the line of scrimmage. The quarterback would lean over close to the ear of the center and call the signal. The center would then go forward and up over the ball. Gene would then step into the vacated spot and repeat the signal clearly for the rest of the team.

Gene would turn and trot up to his position behind the center, followed immediately by the guards and tackles as they took their split positions on the line. The back line would immediately follow the front line with the ends and wingback trotting to their proper positions. The remaining halfback and fullback would move five yards forward to their positions directly back of the quarterback.

This stopped all unauthorized talking in the huddle. I could see from the sidelines those who were talking. Our offensive players by looking straight ahead would not give away the play but out of the corners of their eyes could see the moving of the defensive players in their location.

There was no confusion in either lining up or leaving the huddle to take our offensive positions. Any messengers from the bench would talk to the quarterback before he took his position in the "open huddle."

After our team had used the "open huddle" for three years, one of our good fans named Sam, and a brother of one of our regulars, traveled to Denver, Colorado for a Jaycee Convention. The main speaker at the Convention was Frank Jones, the outstanding head football coach from Notre Dame.

During his message to the Jaycees, he informed them that he was surprising the football world with a new Notre Dame "open huddle." Coach Jones described it exactly as the same "open huddle" we had been using for three years.

"Coach Jones," Sam asked, "would you please diagram your new open huddle on paper for me and explain it to me once again?" Coach Jones very graciously took the time to explain to Sam on paper.

"Coach Jones, our Coldwater High School football coach has used that very same "open huddle" for three years," Sam informed him.

* * *

"Twelve men on the field, twelve men on the field," shouted Joe, the East Lansing football coach!

"Count 'em again Joe, there's only eleven. Too bad you can't count!" I needled him.

The East Lansing and Coldwater teams and coaches were

sitting on the same side of the field, right next to each other. The East Lansing high school football teams had a real live jinx on Coldwater. We never seemed to be able to beat East Lansing. No matter how well we played, every year we would lose.

Annually, East Lansing's team was too powerful for us to play straight power football against. I always tried to invent some legalized trickery to attempt a score against that overpowering, mammoth defense.

This year I had devised a legal sleeper play. After practicing on it many times during the week, I thought we had it down pat. We received the second half kickoff and cleaned up to the left. Our ball carrier was tackled down on the 30 yard line, clear across the field from the players' benches.

As prearranged and instructed, Mac, our end, on the kickoff just trotted up the field near our bench, but remained on the field of play. Our other ten players were clear across the field where the action was with the eleven East Lansing players.

As soon as the ball was declared dead, Mac took off his helmet and rushed over to our huddle hollering as loud as he could, "Leroy out, Leroy out, Leroy out."

Of course Mac meant for our other end Leroy to go out to a wide flanker position near our bench.

Leroy took his helmet off, and slapped the oncoming Mac on the back and shouted: "Go get 'em Mac, go get 'em."

Leroy, carrying his helmet, rushed for the sidelines.

Naturally before he got to the bench, he stopped, and put on his helmet.

His teammates broke out of the huddle, Leroy lined up just inside the sidelines, making sure he was on the line of scrimmage and not offside.

No one on the East Lansing team noticed him --- not even their coach, Joe, nor his substitutes who were close to Leroy.

Gene called for a quick snap, and as Leroy raced down the sidelines unnoticed, the quarterback threw it way across the field to Leroy.

All of East Lansing thought Gene had gone crazy throwing the ball out into empty space, until they saw Leroy gathering the ball in. Unfortunately, Gene's pass was underthrown. Leroy had to wait for the ball, and one of East Lansing's defensive backs who was a sprinter caught Leroy on the ten yard line.

Joe immediately started screaming "Twelve men on the field." However, the officials counted twice and found only eleven. We had not substituted but just changed flankers which was perfectly legal.

* * *

Don was a substitute quarterback whose main asset was his speed, and I used him on special plays. I had come up with a screen pass up the middle. Most coaches used the screen pass to one side or the other.

This screen pass up the middle developed as follows: both guards would pull and block the defensive ends on their respective sides. The tackles and the center would let the defensive linemen through, count three and then move leisurely forward watching the reaction of the line backers, and screen block them as the play developed.

Our offensive ends would do the same and screen block the defensive halfbacks, and our flanker would race down to block the safety. The center would snap the ball between the quarterback's legs directly to our fullback. The fullback would take the snap and run several steps back and jump in the air and rifle the ball over the onrushing lineman to our quarterback who had turned to face the fullback.

The key to the play being successful was getting the ball to the quarterback. He would have to turn dead around and run straight down the middle, as all of our downfield blocking was to the outside.

There was a tendency for Don to be overanxious and start running before he had completely turned around. This would circle him somewhat away from the middle and one of the backer-uppers would get him as our tackle would be blocking him out.

"Don, come here," I shouted at my substitute quarterback. "Go in and call our screen pass up the middle. That defensive line of East Lansing's is ripe for it. They are charging straight in fast. Be sure you make your turn complete upon receiving the ball before you start running down the middle. Now get!"

Don called the play and the center snapped the ball directly to Fry our fullback. Fry ran back, jumped into the air, and rifled the ball to Don. Don, in his excitement circled, and was nailed by a line backer after a two yard gain.

In the meantime, Fry had been slaughtered by five onrushing giant East Lansing defensive linemen. As the charging linemen realized they had been tricked, they lowered the boom on poor Fry.

I immediately pulled Don as Fry struggled to his feet and shook his head. But he was OK.

"Don, what did I tell you about that turn about?" I asked.

"I'm sorry coach," he answered softly.

The next time we had the ball I decided to try again. I once again explained carefully to Don how he had to execute the turn around. Once again Don blew it and circled and was nailed again. Fry took another beating, but remained in the game. The next series of plays when we had the ball, I stubbornly insisted trying Don again.

"Don if you don't execute that turn around properly this time, you are going to walk all the way back to Coldwater," I warned him.

This time Don did it just right and he raced 55 yards for a touchdown right up the middle. I had to take Fry out as he was getting groggy. If only we could have executed right each time, we would have scored three times on that screen pass instead of only once. The touchdown left us one short of winning the game.

Rex, one of our halfbacks, and a great all around football player was also our punter. He went back to punt. The pass from center was high and by the time he came down with it the East Lansing giants were upon him.

However, he got away a tremendous punt of 70 yards from the line of scrimmage. The speedy punt returner for East Lansing sprinted back and took it in the air over his shoulder. After taking three more strides in the wrong direction because of his momentum, he turned and started up field. After he took three steps, "powee", one of our players hit him head on.

Bert, my co-worker exclaimed, "Coach did you see who made that tackle?"

"Yeh, Bert, but I don't believe it," I responded. The jersey number verified that it was Rex, the punter.

Rex threaded his way past the onrushing linemen, and through the entire East Lansing team from 15 yards back of the line of scrimmage. He nailed the punt returner before he had taken three steps forward.

A Michigan State College recruiter was there, and Rex received a football scholarship to Michigan State.

* * *

We always ended the season with our arch rival, Sturgis. Favorites didn't mean much in this rivalry. Upsets occurred 50 percent of the time. This season we had to defeat Sturgis to assure ourselves of a co-championship with East Lansing. If Sturgis won they would be the co-champions with East Lansing.

The day of the game, it started pouring rain early and continued right through the noon hour. After dinner, the Sturgis coach and athletic director called me. He asked if I would agree to postpone the game until Monday.

Even though I thought we were really mentally prepared to play that night, I readily agreed that it made sense to postpone this important game for better weather. Not only would good weather provide better quality of play, but it would make for a real good gate. The money was needed for the Sturgis Athletic Association.

Monday night was a beautiful football night, and we played before a huge crowd. Not only were all the Coldwater and Sturgis fans there, but nearby fans from other towns came over to watch this all important clash for the championship on this "off" playing night.

Joe, our fullback, broke loose early in the game on a trap block up the middle and ran 65 yards to the one yard line. Although Joe had broken into the clear, he and his 245 pounds had somewhat run out of gas. The safety man for Sturgis nailed him on the one yard line.

I knew we would score with Gene taking it across on a quarterback sneak. This would reduce the chance of a fumble or penalty which could be the only logical thing to keep us from scoring. I decided not to take any chances, I wanted this early touchdown to give us the lead.

"Callahan, come here," I shouted at one of my substitute guards.

Callahan was a real competitor, and a smart kid.

"You go in and tell Gene to take it over on a quarterback sneak," I said to him.

"Be sure to tell the team, I don't in any way want anyone offside on this play, do you understand?"

"Yeh, Coach," Callahan verified.

Callahan raced in and called the play. Just as I knew, Gene had no trouble carrying the pigskin across the goal line. But down went the flag. Callahan was offside, and we never did score on that series of plays.

With two minutes to go we scored the go ahead touchdown. On the following kickoff I was real anxious to get my tackles down fast, and prevent a runback. I was exhorting them from the sidelines. As the ball was kicked, I watched to see how fast all eleven took off except Gene, who was held back purposely to prevent someone from breaking loose and going all the way.

However, right in front of me was my star end. As the other players sprinted down the field, Pete stood still looking up in the stands. I don't know what was going through his mind but I knew what was going through mine.

I rushed out across the sidelines, turned him downfield with my hands, and gave him a swift kick in the seat and screamed at him. He took off, but quick. We won the game and our co-championship.

* * *

Several seasons later, we were having a very mediocre season. Battle Creek Lakeview had been rated the number one team in the entire state for the year. We were scheduled to play them near the end of the season. Our plan for three weeks was toward an upset of this number one team, knowing that such an upset would give us a successful season.

The big night arrived and we were ready. We were champing at the bit with the adrenalin flowing. Besides being mentally prepared, we had every detail of strategy planned and practiced. Nothing had been left undone to pull this upset of the season in the state.

The entire game went as planned and with four minutes to go in the fourth quarter, we were ahead 6 to 0. However, I knew that Lakeview's all state halfback, Holburt, could shake loose at any time and go all the way.

We had the ball at this time and had driven all the way to the 25 yard line of Lakeview. As we approached their goal-line the going became tougher. On third down and ten, I decided to use one of our trick plays. If we could score now, we would have the game wrapped up. I called time out, and sent the play in with one of my substitutes.

We ran the setup play making only two yards, and then went immediately into our trick play without a huddle. It was a play of organized confusion. We had players running every which way. The Lakeview defense was caught by surprise.

All of our players arrived at the same time at their pre-designated locations, and paused for one second. The offensive linemen as well as our entire team stood straight up without taking a normal stance.

The center snapped the ball, the quarterback took three quick steps back, the offensive linemen just stood in front of an opponent, and the ends and backs were running all over the place. Our passer threw a quick pass to one end who was streaking down the sidelines. He gathered the ball in and raced 23 yards for the score. It put us ahead 12 to 0 and sewed up the game.

The Lakeview defensive players were still in a daze, but so were the officials. When I planned to use special trick legal plays in a game, I never could decide whether to alert the officials before the game or not. I decided against it, because in one game when I had alerted them, they inadvertently gave it away.

The head linesman, Smitty, called the play back. When Smitty got excited, he would stutter badly. I raced out onto the field and confronted him. I knew the play had been executed legally. We had practiced it for three weeks, dozens and dozens of times just for this one occasion, and it went off exactly as planned.

"Smitty, there is nothing wrong with that play, there is no way you can call that play back," I screamed at him!

"Tu, tuh, tuh, tuh, tuh, twelve men on the field, Flu, Flue, Floy, Floyd," he stuttered.

"Count 'em, count 'em, count 'em," I screamed.

Both officials counted eleven.

By this time I was screaming at both officials.

"Award us our six rightful points now!" I demanded.

The Lakeview coach was in a daze, also. But he was insisting that it was an illegal play even though he didn't have any idea what was going on and what had happened.

When the official Smitty had been convinced that only eleven Coldwater players had been involved, he searched for another reason to call the play illegal. "The, the, the, the offensive linemen wer, wer, wer, not dow, down, down on thr, thr, three po, po, po, points," he finally got out.

"Baloney, Baloney, Baloney," I shouted into his face. "The offensive linemen do not have to be down on three points. All that is required is to be on the line of scrimmage, and pause for one second before the ball is snapped." I always studied the rules when devising a new trick play.

"The linemen weren't su, su, su, set for one su, su, su, second," Smitty stuttered.

"I know they were," I screamed. "I watched them particularly for this, and we practiced it fifty times. I always made them pause over a second."

All my pleading did no good. Smitty still called the play back and disallowed our six points.

Lakeview took the ball over on their 23 yard line, with 3 minutes to go. We held them to two yards the next two plays. With time running out, and 3rd down and eight, Holburt slipped over our left tackle, broke loose and went 75 yards for the winning touchdown, beating us 7 to 6.

I knew the game was lost as soon as I saw Holburt break into the open field because we had no speed to catch him. In my frustration of losing such an important game and feeling we had been robbed of the upset of the year, I grabbed the phones and hollered up to the press box to one of my coaches.

"What hole did he hit, what hole did he hit?"

Bob answered, "I don't know but he sure went a long way, didn't he?"

* * *

We not only had trouble with East Lansing on the football field, but we sometimes had trouble with them off the field. It was near the end of the season, and we had a very important game with East Lansing at Coldwater. Not only was it important to us in the league standings but we also expected a huge crowd which was going to make us well financially in our Coldwater High School athletic association.

We were dependent entirely upon our gate receipts for all our expenses. We did not ask for, nor did we receive any help from the school board. If our gates were down, we then had to go without many things. All we needed to guarantee a huge crowd for this East Lansing game was good weather.

It started raining the night before the game, and continued

all the next morning. At noon I drove down to the field. It was flooded; a quagmire of mud. I called the weather man, and he promised rain the rest of the day and into the night.

I talked to my principal and decided the game should be postponed. I called the State Athletic Association and talked with the state director. I told him the situation, and he agreed with our thinking.

He gave me permission to play it on the following Monday even though we and East Lansing had games the following Friday. I also received permission to play the game on the Friday night following the end of the regular season. Of course, we could also make up the game the next night on Saturday.

Armed with this information, I called the East Lansing football coach, Joe. Although he would rather play the game as scheduled, he agreed that it made sense to postpone it because of the playing conditions, and also for our material needs.

Joe checked with his athletic director, and agreed to the postponement. At the time, they didn't want to choose the date, but would agree later on one of the two available dates. They could not play the next night, Saturday, because of a special school commitment.

I called the area newspapers and radio to publish special bulletins postponing the game until a later date due to inclement weather. I called and cancelled the officials, and notified our student body over the intercom. I scheduled a workout in the gym after school for my squad in case East Lansing decided to play Monday night.

Just before school let out, I called Joe at East Lansing to find out if they had made up their minds yet on what date they desired. If it was to be Monday night I needed to know so I could notify the papers, radio, and the officials.

I could not get hold of Joe or the athletic director so I asked to speak to the Superintendent, Mr. Chambers. I asked Mr. Chambers if I could get in touch with Joe or the athletic director.

Mr. Chambers curtly notified me that neither one of them

were available as they had left with the football squad for Coldwater to play the game. I was amazed.

"Mr. Chambers, you, Joe, and the athletic director know that the game at Coldwater has been postponed. Why would they be making the trip?"

"We decided that we were not going to postpone it, but play it tonight," he responded.

"You mean to tell me that you decided to play it, after you agreed to the postponement? Then not even let us know about your change of mind?" I asked in amazement.

"I never agreed to the postponement in the first place," he answered.

"But your coach and athletic director agreed," I said.

"I have the ultimate decision," he continued. "I didn't think it was necessary to notify you. It is your responsibility to fulfill the signed contract we have with you."

I couldn't believe my ears. "Mr. Chambers, I don't believe that Joe and your football squad have left yet. It is only 3:10. If they haven't, you better let them know right now that there will not be a game played tonight at Coldwater," I informed him. "If they have left, I recommend you have the state police stop them and notify them at Charlotte." We hung up.

I assumed this would be the end of our problem for tonight. I now had the feeling that we might have future problems in scheduling the game for makeup. I knew that the Superintendent had stepped in and was the one causing the trouble.

I called the State Director and told him the situation. I asked him if we had to play the game tonight because of our contract.

"Absolutely not," he answered. "You are the host school and the authority rests in your hands to determine if the weather is such to be a problem with the players, officials, and the fans."

I worked my squad out in the gym after school, and then went home for supper. I had just started eating when the phone rang.

It was Charlie, our chief custodian, "Coach, the East

Lansing football squad is here and want in the locker room to dress for the game tonight. I told them the game had been postponed, but they said it hadn't, and they were here to play."

"Charlie, did you let them in the locker room?" I asked.

"No, I didn't let them in. They said they would dress in the bus and would be ready for the kickoff at 7:30 p.m.," Charlie answered.

I jumped into my car and drove down to Waterworks Park and the football field. Upon my arrival, I found the big Greyhound bus, and the football squad in the bus. There were also several cars with the cheerleaders and some fans including the athletic director and the superintendent. By this time the rain had let up, but the field was still a quagmire of mud.

I got out of my car, and strode up to Joe, the East Lansing Coach, and asked, "What in the dickens is going on here anyway, Joe?"

Joe looked sheepish, but answered softly, "We are here to play the game, Floyd."

Even as mad as I was, I felt sorry for Joe because I knew he had been pressured into this situation by his superintendent, and really didn't have much to say about it.

"Joe, if it wasn't for the strained relations that this will cause between our two schools, it would be the most humorous event of my coaching career," I stated.

I did not talk to the superintendent. I could see no point in it at this time. "Joe, I would just like to ask you one question, why didn't you let me know when you changed your minds?"

"I left that up to my boss, the superintendent. He said he would take care of everything." I knew Joe had been instructed in just what to say and do.

At exactly 7:20 the squad, fully dressed, poured out of the Greyhound bus, and performed some calisthenics at the end of the field in the dark. At 7:30, game time, the starting eleven lined up for the kickoff. The kicker kicked the ball off the mud where the 40 yard line might have been.

All eleven ran down through the mud to the darker end of the field and located the ball in the mud and fell on it. All eleven of them trotted back with the muddy ball to the bus where the cheerleaders lead a victory cheer, and then the players loaded back into the bus.

Joe came over to me and said, "Floyd we are now claiming a 2 to 0 forfeit."

"Congratulations, Joe," I remarked sarcastically. I really was flabbergasted as I stood in the rain and watched the big bus drive away followed by four cars.

As I left for home, I couldn't help but wonder how much the East Lansing officials had taught those players that night that would help them become outstanding citizens.

Even though we did everything in our power to try and get East Lansing to make up the game, they steadfastly refused. Their answer was that they had already won the game by forfeit, and we were taking the case to the State Athletic Association to make it official in their record.

It took several weeks for the State Association to set up a hearing date, and for each school to prepare their case. By the time the hearing rolled around, we were into the basketball season, and we were to play East Lansing in basketball at Coldwater within two weeks of the hearing date.

At this time the country was involved in a long coal workers' strike. There was talk about closing the schools. We were going to be unable to heat the school. We were heating with coal, and the electric company was going to cut off our electricity because of the lack of coal in their stock to produce enough electricity.

The State Director of Athletics requested the head football coaches, the athletic directors, the principals, and the East Lansing superintendent to be present at the hearing. The hearing was to take place before the State Athletic Executive Committee in the Capitol building in Lansing, Michigan.

As I was also the coach and athletic director, only my principal, Mr. Brady, and I had to come from Coldwater. However, four were requested from East Lansing, including the head coach, athletic director, principal, and the superintendent, Mr. Chambers, because he had been particularly involved.

When we met at the hearing, East Lansing left Joe, the football coach, at school. I felt this was on purpose so Joe wouldn't be present to verify our agreement to postpone the game.

Mr. Chambers, the superintendent, presented the East Lansing case, asking for an official forfeit for the record. He based their case on the fact that they had not ultimately agreed to postpone the game. That their school calendar was so crowded with activities that it would be impossible to find a date to make the game up.

They had called a friend in the Coldwater area, and had him check the condition of our field in the late afternoon. The friend reported the condition of the field wasn't so bad, and the rain was letting up.

Therefore, East Lansing felt that Eby was putting the crowd and his athletic finances ahead of East Lansing's activity calendar. After all, the Big Ten never postponed a football game because of weather.

I presented our case. It had rained throughout the previous night and all forenoon the day of the game. Because of the newspapers deadlines and officials, I had to make the decision one way or another by noon which would also help the visiting team to make necessary arrangements, such as cancelling the chartered bus.

The weather man also forecast rain the rest of the day and night, clearing up on Saturday morning. I admitted the weather man had been partially wrong, as it started letting up in the late afternoon.

"In answer to Mr. Chamber's charge that we are interested in crowds and gate receipts I plead guilty," I remarked. "I know when we play a game in the rain, our crowd and finances are nil. When we play in decent weather, we have huge crowds and money to keep our athletic program going."

"I also believe that if the weather is so bad that people will not come and sit through the game, then the weather is too bad for the players to play in," I continued.

"I am disappointed that the East Lansing football coach isn't here. According to my communication from the State, he was to have been here. I think it is important to this committee to have the East Lansing Coach verify our agreement to postpone the game."

The state director spoke. "Mr. Chambers, why isn't your football coach here? We requested you to bring him."

Mr. Chambers countered, "Our coach had some very important classes at the school, and we didn't believe we needed him to adequately present our case."

"Mr. Chambers, you call your Coach right now and tell him to get to this meeting just as soon as he can," The state director demanded!

The meeting was held up until Joe arrived. I then continued to present my case: "In attempting to find an available date to make up the game, East Lansing gave me the following reasons:

The next night, Saturday, was out of the question because of an important social function at the East Lansing high school. The following Monday was not agreeable because they would be playing two games within five days which the state association would not allow. I had already told them that the state association had given us special permission.

The following Friday after the end of the season was not convenient, because they believed their athletes should have a full week off before they started basketball and wrestling."

I continued, "I am sure one of the three could have been somewhat satisfactory in the interest of cooperation. I know Coldwater would be willing to cooperate with East Lansing or any other school in the league, under these same circumstances. In fact several years ago, Sturgis asked us to do the same as we asked East Lansing to do. We readily agreed and Sturgis had a huge crowd, and their athletic fund was greatly enriched."

Joe verified our earlier agreement, although you could tell he was under pressure from his superintendent.

I concluded my case, "We play East Lansing in basketball

in two weeks at Coldwater. We may be forced to close our school and gym, because of the coal strike which will take our heat and lights. It is entirely possible that this might happen all over the country. If this happens at Coldwater, am I expected to ask East Lansing to postpone our basketball game? Or should I hang up kerosene lanterns, put earmuffs, coats, and gloves on the players, and go ahead with the game? Do you suppose East Lansing will want to check our coal bin to make sure we are out of coal or would they take our word for it?"

The Committee turned down East Lansing's request for an official forfeit declaring it a "no contest." However, the state director and committee members really chewed the East Lansing officials out.

The state director said, "Mr. Chambers, we think it is despicable the way you and your school have acted in this situation. Your action is strictly uncalled for. We reprimand you for your lack of cooperation. We hope that your attitude from now on will be different, and be in the sense of fair play and cooperation. We commend Coldwater on the handling of this situation."

The Twin Valley also reprimanded East Lansing at our next league meeting. Even though we had been completely exonerated, we still lost. We lost the opportunity of playing the game and our athletic association lost the gate receipts. We felt the financial pinch for two years, but we survived.

Praise God, Joe and I remained friends.

"For by Him were all things created,
that are in earth, visible and invisible,
whether they are thrones, or
dominions, or principalities, or
powers --- all things were created by
Him, and for Him"
Colossians 1:16

THE CREATION OF
A BASKETBALL DYNASTY

"Time out, time out, time out," screamed the Eaton Rapids coach as he jumped off the bench. "What's going on here anyway, Eby?" he shouted at me as he approached our bench. "This isn't basketball."

"On that last play one of your guys knocked my shooter clear through the locker-room doors and into the girl's locker room! If this keeps up, I'll have to call a doctor and an ambulance," he yelled.

The game was only three minutes old and we were already ahead 10 to zip. Eaton Rapids didn't seem to know what had hit them with our new style of race horse basketball. This was the first time they had played us, although we had been scouted the year before by Coach Stephens. This was our opening game of the season, being played in our small gym.

We swept them off their feet, and won 50 to 19. A few minutes after the game as the two teams were showering,

Coach Stephens came to me.

"Eby, in all of my years of coaching, I have never seen anything like this. Most of my starters are black and blue from the beating they took, and most of my players are afraid to come out of the locker room even now."

"Oh come on, Coach," I answered. "You're putting me on. We are just playing our natural brand of ball. We may be a little rough because of the opening game but we will smooth out in a few weeks."

* * *

The previous year, as I had come back from World War II and the United States Navy, we had an excellent team, winning the league championship for the first time in many years. This first post war team was short on basketball ability, but it was made up of a real bunch of scrappers and competitors. Our new style of race horse basketball paid off in championship dividends as it took advantage of the aggressiveness of this hard working group of players.

However, we were upset in the district tournament by Sturgis 29 to 28 in a barn burner.

Now in this opener with Eaton Rapids, we were attempting to put together another championship season. We did just that by winning 14 straight league games, and losing only one non-conference game. We had very little trouble winning the district championship, defeating Kalamazoo State High 52 to 28 and Three Rivers 63 to 41.

We drubbed South Haven 45 to 27 in the opening game of the regionals, and then played St. Joseph in the regional finals. St. Joseph was a team of great tournament tradition having won the State Championships several times, and were always tough at tournament time.

With 48 seconds left to play we were leading St. Joseph 35 to 34. Tighe intercepted a St. Joseph pass and threw it to Corless on the fast break. Corless, although only a sophomore, was an excellent player. I just knew he was going to put in this dog shot and sew up the game for us.

1948 team preparing mentally for another game.

Just as he went up for the lay-up, an opposing player crashed him from behind, and knocked him into the end bleachers. Although he missed the shot, I was sure he would make the free throws.

However, in the excitement, the officials failed to make the call, even though Corless had to climb out of the laps of fans located in the end bleachers.

With seven seconds to go, we fouled a St. Joe shooter, and he made the two free throws and won the game. The St. Joe Coach came into our funeral-like locker room, and congratulated us on our fine play.

He volunteered, "I just told my boys that we have just won the state championship, as we have beaten the best team in the state. There is not another team in the state that can beat us."

How prophetic he was as no one came within ten points of beating St. Joseph in the next three games as they won the state championship. This should have made us feel better, but it didn't as we now realized how close we came to winning it ourselves.

If it hadn't been for the last missed shot, or the officials' error in not calling the foul, or Jon only making one shot out of eighteen? Forget it, Eby, we lost. No excuses!

* * *

The next season, we once again opened with Eaton Rapids, and Coach Stephens was still unhappy as we drubbed them again 65 to 30. Coach Stephens was sorry they had signed a two year contract with us, but this really did end our playing days with Eaton Rapids.

It looked like we were on the way again to a championship season, but in the first league game we were beaten by Albion 51 to 50. We rebounded against Battle Creek Lakeview the next week 60 to 35. The next week found us playing our bitter rivals, Marshall, in their cracker box of a gym.

We were behind 40 to 26 with three minutes and five seconds remaining in the game. The scoreboard had broken down, and the Marshall official was keeping time at the scorer's table with a little red stop clock.

During a time out, I went up to the bench and asked him how much time was left on the clock. The clock was pointed directly to him and I couldn't see it.

He curtly replied, "You take care of your coaching, and I will take care of the time keeping."

I bristled. "Listen, I want to know how much time there is left in this game, and you are going to tell me."

"I will tell you when the time is up and the game is over," he replied sarcastically.

However, I did find out that there were just 3 minutes and 5 seconds left.

Our cause appeared hopeless. The Marshall Redskins fans, coaches, and scoring officials were savouring the victory over the defending champs. They were all enjoying it immensely.

Many of our Coldwater fans had already disappointedly left the crowded Marshall gym. The boos and catcalls were becoming louder by the minute. The fans were already celebrating the victory over Coach Eby and his cocky Cardinals.

It didn't help matters any as I kept sending my co-worker Bob up to the scorer's table every few seconds to check the remaining time. Bob didn't take any of their contempt, and always came back with the time.

During the time out I instructed my players. "We haven't played any ball all night, and it is about time to start. If we are really champions, we will have the competitiveness to come back. Throw all caution to the wind, and start pressing tight even if we foul out."

We won 46 to 42. Everyone in the gym was mad at us except the few Coldwater fans who were faithful to the end. We were lucky to get out alive. The timer was really upset with us as Bob kept his eye on him the entire last 3 minutes.

* * *

From that game on we really started rolling, winning game after game by lopsided scores. We had our third consecutive league championships almost sewn up as we traveled to East Lansing, to meet the Trojans on their own court. They stopped our winning steak 41 to 40. However, by drubbing Adrian and Hillsdale, we won the championship outright.

We won the district tourney by defeating Sturgis and Kalamazoo State High. At the first game of the regionals we met the defending state champions... the same St. Joseph team that defeated us by one point a year earlier on their way to the state championship.

At halftime St. Joe was ahead of us 26 to 18. I had just about had it, trying to think of what we could do to turn this game around. It was unthinkable to have St. Joe beat us two years in a row and go on to win another state championship.

"Fellows," I said in the locker room, "in ten years of

coaching I have never been so discouraged as I am now. St. Joe has slowed our fast break down to a walk, and we are playing right into their hands, as we have quit trying to run. We have subconsciously settled back satisfied to play them at their own game. We will never beat a St. Joe team playing their game.

"I am so discouraged thinking about the state championship they took away from us last year. They are doing the very same thing this year. I just can't take it. If we lose this game, this will be the last basketball game I will ever coach.

"I want you to start pressing tight -- race horsing every time we have the ball. Make things happen that will speed up the tempo of the game. Don't let us give it to them on a silver platter. Let's make 'em earn it."

From that point on St. Joe was doomed.

We outscored them 19 to 5 in the third quarter, and won the game going away 48 to 39. We won the regional championship by swamping South Haven 56 to 40 which qualified us for the state quarter finals.

Alma had been rated number one in the state during nearly the entire season. They were favorites to win and succeed St. Joe as the state champions. Alma was our opponent in the state quarter finals in Lansing.

Undoubtedly Alma was the best team we had played all season, but we had a good night and defeated them handily. We led by as much as 17 points in the third quarter, and ended up winning 51 to 42. The Detroit Free Press had picked the wrong team.

The quarter finals were on Wednesday, and after the Alma game I sent the team home on the bus with Bob my co-worker. I stayed to scout the second game. We were to play the winners on Friday night in the semi-finals of the state.

In the second game, Grand Rapids Godwin Heights defeated Davidson. Godwin had a super star playing center. Spencer was 6 foot seven inches tall, which was a real giant in those days.

Even though he was somewhat impressive against Davidson, I really didn't believe we would have too much trouble with him. Our tallest player was only 6 feet 1 inch, but I felt our race horse tactics would tire Spencer until he would end up ineffective.

Most of our Coldwater fans stayed and watched the second game also. Their impressions of Spencer were the same as mine. The only difference is that I kept mine to myself and the fans told my players when they got home.

Friday we left by school bus to Lansing where we planned to stay until Sunday, win or lose. We were staying in the Hotel Olds.

On the opening jump ball with Godwin, I jumped Sowles against Spencer. Sowles was my shortest starter at 5 feet 5 inches. I admit it looked quite ridiculous jumping against a 6 feet 7 inch center.

Most people thought I was doing it as a show, but it was part of my strategy. I knew we had no one who could come close to outjumping Spencer so I kept my height where it could be used in retrieving the ball as we gambled on the jump. Sowles jumped as high as he could, but it appeared he was less than half way up to the giant.

Our team was mentally down, probably due to our peak playing against Alma. Also the influence of our fans' opinions about the lousy Godwin team as they looked against Davidson. Certainly, Godwin had to be a good team as they had lost only two games all year.

We struggled all night against the giant and his teammates. Only Sowles, my small guard, was really hustling. The rest of the players seemed to be dead on their feet.

We were behind 35 to 34 with less than two minutes to go, and Godwin had control of the ball. Fry, our center, stole the ball and dribbled the length of the court and laid it up, putting us ahead 36 to 35. Godwin brought the ball down and lost it out of bounds.

I immediately called time out with a minute and 20 seconds to go in the game. We were not a stalling team. In

Coach Eby with Rex Corless, All State - All Class - three consecutive years. A real super star in all sports.

fact I didn't believe in stalling. I had seen as many games lost as won by stalling.

However, the previous week, we had worked on a special stall. Corless our superstar positioned himself out court near the center line. He threw it in to Sowles who in turn passed it to Corless near the center. Corless spread his legs wide apart and held the ball out in front of him sort of teasing Godwin to come and get it.

When Corless's defensive man would approach, Corless would draw it back between his legs where the defensive man couldn't touch it. If they double teamed him, he would fake and drive out of the mess and pass off to one of our other players.

Then Corless would reposition himself. Our players would give him the ball again so he would once again have his dribble left. He repeated the entire procedure again. We were able to use this procedure for the full 80 seconds and stalled the game out. We won 36 to 35.

Even though we won, I was real uptight with my team and myself as I felt that we had almost given away the state championship. We were not mentally prepared for the game. I vowed to myself at the end of that game that no way were we going to be mentally down the next night in the state finals including myself. River Route was playing Ishpeming in the second game and we were playing the winners in the finals for the state championship.

After the players showered, I loaded them into the school bus and drove them back to the Hotel Olds.

Before they got out of the bus, I spoke to them. "Fellows, we were just plain lucky. We didn't really deserve that win over Godwin tonight. We almost threw the state championship right out the window, because we weren't mentally prepared for this game. We were standing flat-footed, we were not hustling on the press and we were not fast-breaking.

"I want you to hear this and I want you to get it straight. I am giving you just ten minutes after you leave this bus to go to your room.

"No one --- but no one --- is to leave his room until 9:00 in the morning. No one is to be in any other room except his own. If you want something to eat, you call the team manager's room and have Carlos go get what you want. Don't one of you step across your threshold into the hall, but let Carlos come into your room.

"I may scout River Rouge for one quarter, or the entire game or maybe not at all. I may come back at any time.

"If anyone is violating my instructions, I am sending you back to Coldwater on the next commercial bus. The only way you will see the game tomorrow will be to pay your way in because you will not be dressing with the squad.

"Do you understand that or not? Now get to your rooms! We will meet in my room tomorrow at 9:10 a.m. I don't want to see a smile on any of you all day tomorrow!"

I went back to the gym to scout River Rouge and Ishpeming, feeling quite safe that I could stay for the whole game. Some of the players' girl friends came to the hotel to see them and found them already in their rooms. The girls called them on the hotel phone, and the boys told them all to get out of the hotel, but quick.

We had our squad meeting in my room the next morning at 9:10. I then outlined our program for the entire day. We started off with a good breakfast, and followed our schedule precisely, including a light meal at noon.

At 4:00 p.m. we traveled in our school bus to East Lansing to eat a meal in a restaurant before our championship game with River Rouge that night.

* * *

Of course, during the entire tournament trail, I had used the same clothes, socks, shirt, tie, suit, shoes, etc. My wife would clean the same clothes after each game. I cannot say that I was really superstitious, but I just didn't want to take any chances.

Bert, my co-worker, told me early in my coaching career, "Coach, always get your haircut the day of the game. If you lose the game, you won't have to listen to that mularkey for a couple of weeks. By that time you may have won a game before you have to go to the barbershop again."

I therefore had made it a practice to have my haircuts on the day of a game.

I went to my barber, Lyle, for a haircut on the day that we were going to play our first game in the district tournament.

As I paid Lyle, he volunteered, "Coach, if you win tonight, you come back and get you a free haircut before the next game. We want to go all the way this year."

We won six straight games in two weeks. I received six

free haircuts from Lyle. After winning the Godwin game we stayed in Lansing. I missed my free haircut the next day as we were preparing to play River Rouge that night for the championship.

I was too nervous to eat. As the players and my co-worker ate a meal in East Lansing at 4:30 p.m., I thought I would use this time to sneak off to a barber shop and get my lucky haircut. I located a shop with six barbers. I walked in and sat down in one of the barber chairs.

"What do you want?" the barber asked.

I sure didn't look like I needed a haircut after six in two weeks including the last one yesterday.

"I want a haircut," I answered.

"What for?" He was puzzled.

I attempted to explain to him and the rest of the shop what it was all about.

"We are playing River Rouge tonight for the state championship. I need a lucky haircut to make sure we win. Just give me a trim," I explained.

The barber trimmed me for sure. He charged me double of what I would normally pay in Coldwater. Thinking he might do it for free because of so little time needed, I was shocked and somewhat uptight about the charge.

"Here is your money," I said. "But if we get beaten by River Rouge tonight, I am coming back for a refund."

He looked at me in surprise. "If you get beat, you come back and I will give it back," he said.

I was giving my players final instructions just before sending them out of the locker room and on to the court to play River Rouge.

I was interrupted by a loud commotion down the locker room hall. I looked down the hall, and saw a man with a black bag come rushing down the hall directly at me and the team. He was being chased by two security guards.

It was my barber, Lyle, and he shouted to me. "Coach, I got my equipment in this bag, and we have ɔ give you that lucky haircut. Just come over right now by this electric plug and it will only take a few minutes. We just don't dare to take a chance."

The security guards were ready to throw Lyle out on his ear.

"Hey," I shouted at them, "Leave him alone, he is my friend."

The guards left. I explained to Lyle how I had already received my lucky game haircut that afternoon.

"You sure that will do it Coach?" Lyle asked.

"Yeh, Lyle," I answered. "It will do the job, but I really thank you for your concern and effort."

That seemed to satisfy Lyle. He went to his seat to watch, fearful that another barber would bring bad luck.

* * *

The players were warming up on the same mammoth Jenison Field House at Michigan State as the one we played on ten years before when Williamston won the state championship.

As I was standing by our bench along the sidelines near the center of the court, one of our fanatic fans, a businessman in Coldwater handed me an envelope. I stuck the envelope in the inner pocket of my suit coat and forgot about it.

What an exciting time it was to be playing for the state championship before such a huge crowd. I was all nerves, adrenalin, and just plain scared. I was glad that my players were not as scared as I was.

We had to win it, I thought; for second place is just not good enough. People only remember the champions, not the runner-ups. Come on guys, let's put it all together tonight.

At the end of the first quarter we were ahead 11 to 10. Midway through the second quarter, I was stunned when our superstar, Corless, sprained an ankle. He had to be helped into the locker room where our team physician would diagnose the extent of the injury.

What a time to lose a superstar. Corless had been all state in all classes for three consecutive years. One of the best in

1949 State Championship team battles for the "win" against River Rouge. Corless is shooting, Cox and McConnell moving to rebound positions.

the entire state, especially in playing race horse basketball.

Why, oh why, now? "Come on Mac," I told McConnell on the bench. "It's really up to you, now."

I had a lot of faith in Mac. He was an excellent player. Many times during the year, he had carried the load because he could go in for almost any position. However, I rationalized, no way can we replace Corless in this all-important game.

At half time we were still leading 22 to 18. The doctor had taped up Corless's ankle. He said he could play, but indicated that it would definitely cut his effectiveness.

The River Rouge coach had scouted us well, and especially Corless. Coach Green had his defensive man play Corless five feet loose. He knew Corless very seldom shot out court but nearly always drove for the bucket or for a quick, short jump shot.

THE CREATION OF A BASKETBALL DYNASTY/99

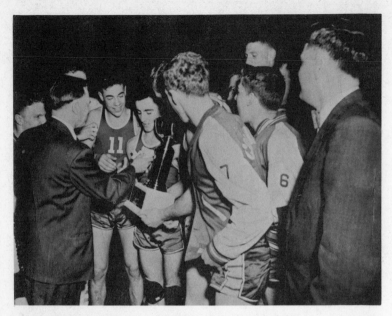

Receiving the 1949 State Championship Trophy on the court following the games from Assistant State Athletic Director.

Even with his bad ankle, and River Rouge's most talented defensive man playing him loose, Corless scored 18 points in less than three quarters which is comparable to 40 points in a game today.

Because of his ankle, Corless fouled out as he couldn't move as quickly in the press. Mac went in and finished the game in great style.

In the first two minutes of the final quarter, we spurted ahead 39 to 26 and sewed up the game. The final score was 49 to 42 with Coldwater winning their first state championship.

After the picture taking, and after receiving the large state championship trophy and a jubilant shower in the locker room, we greeted our friends who came in to congratulate us, including Lyle, the barber.

I instructed the boys to meet at the south end of the field house. I told them that as soon as I could, I would drive them back downtown. After taking care of my duties with the press and radio interviews, I located my squad at the south end of the arena.

Naturally, all their girl friends were with them, having a great time. After ruling the squad quite rigidly all season, the girls were still somewhat worried about my reaction. As I approached the group, I could feel some fear along with the excitement.

"Hey gals, it is good to see you with my players, and sharing in our good fortune," I greeted them. "How about loading in the bus with the players and letting me drive you all downtown to Lansing together.

"We will cancel all curfews and rules. I just ask all of you to be ladies and gentlemen. I am proud of all of you, including your girl friends."

You could see that they could hardly believe their ears, but they were all now celebrating in a noisy bus. What a glad, jubilant, noisy bus ride, I thought as I drove the school bus through the traffic and stopped at the Hotel Olds. At this point I cut the boys and girls loose, after mutually agreeing with them on a reasonable curfew.

* * *

The next morning, Sunday, I allowed the squad to sleep until 9:30. We then went to breakfast, and to a Church in Lansing as a group.

While I was waiting for the boys to get up, I took the elevator down to the lobby to buy a newspaper. I rode the elevator with two gentlemen I didn't know. I believe they were college coaches, at the tournament to scout for prospects.

They were talking to each other as I silently listened.

"Did you see that Coldwater team last night?" one asked the other.

"I sure did," the other replied. "I have never seen

anything like it. They ran all over the court hawking the ball, throwing long passes, fast breaking constantly, and driving and shooting like mad."

"It sure was something to see."

As I left the elevator, I felt good. I did feel somewhat bad for the River Rouge coach, Loften Greene, because I knew we had beaten a good team and an excellent coach. Time proved me to be right. Loften and I became good friends. He became one of the greatest basketball coaches of all time and his record proved it.

* * *

Just before we went to breakfast, I reached inside my suit coat pocket and accidentally found the envelope that our fanatic Coldwater fan had given to me just before the opening jump in the Rouge game. It was a scouting report on River Rouge that the businessman himself had written up on Rouge.

It also told me just what to do to beat Rouge. Although I had not opened it until the morning after the game, I am sure this fan felt he provided the victory with his personalized scouting report and his sound instructions.

Oh, well, we need to praise God for our fans. Without fans, it would be a mighty dull game.

After church, we ate a good dinner, and headed the school bus toward Coldwater. Six miles north of Coldwater, we were met by a large caravan of cars loaded with fans. The caravan escorted us into Coldwater and through town.

School was called off on Monday and the day was reserved for a parade and celebration. Thousands of people lined the streets as the team, coaches, and cheerleaders were given rides in open convertibles followed by a program of recognition.

After several weeks of unusual excitement --- of publicity, banquets, and parties --- the community, school and players returned to normal.

Victory parade following return home from State finals.

Coach Eby and co-Captains Sowles and Cox receiving ride in convertible in parade. Followed by other members of State Champions squad.

Coach Eby and his two co-captains receiving the key to the city.

During the summer season, I was making definite plans for next basketball season to win another league, district, regional and state championship. We had four of our top six men coming back. We had to replace our big man, the center, Leroy Cox. However, we already had the replacement groomed and ready, and his name was Bernie.

Bernie was 6 feet 2 inches, and could really jump. He was just what our team needed, a big man who could control the boards and start our fast break. Our other players had all the other needed abilities to win championships, even though they were all small.

Midway in the previous season I had brought Bernie up from the reserves when one of our starters suffered knee trouble. Bernie filled the bill immediately. When Jim came back to the lineup, Bernie filled in anywhere and anytime we needed him. His play convinced us that he would be our needed big man next year.

In the late spring of our state championship year, Bernie's parents moved to Indiana. Without any pushing from me, Bernie and his folks made the decision to leave him here to finish out his last year. One of our fine citizens and his wife had offered him their home and meals for the year.

I was overjoyed to know that he was going to be with us to win more championships the next year. Even though I was reluctant to do so, I felt led to talk to Bernie.

"Bernie, I really want you to stay. But I want to be sure what is best for you. I suggest you move with your parents this summer, and see how you like it down there. At the end of the summer, if you still want to come back here, we will be happy to have you."

Bernie was not only a great athlete, but an excellent, well-behaved kid, and an excellent student.

"I will do that coach," Bernie said. "But I will be back in time to enroll at Coldwater High."

I thought, "I surely hope so, because if he doesn't, there goes our championship out the window."

The middle of August, Bernie called me. "Coach, I really don't like it down here. I want to come back to Coldwater to graduate and play sports."

"Great, Bernie," I shouted in the phone. "We really want you."

When I arrived home from coaching school the last week of August, I had a message to call Bernie.

"This is Coach Eby, when are you coming, Bernie?"

"Coach," he whimpered, half crying, "I really want to come, but I guess I can't now. The basketball coach and principal, when I told them I was going back to Coldwater, told me I would have to enroll at their school right now.

"If I didn't I couldn't ever enroll during the year even if I wanted to come to be with my folks after basketball season. Also that my folks now live in their district, and I will have to finish my education here!"

The coach and principal had watched Bernie practice basketball during the summer and realized his great basketball potential. They decided they would go all out to keep him there.

Bernie played basketball at their school, and even though he was the shortest starter at 6-2, he was their leading scorer.

Later on Bernie became a physics instructor at a

University in a distant state. Everytime he stops in to see me, he tells me how much he regrets not coming back, and listening to those men badgering him into staying.

Naturally, I was very disappointed. I still felt good about doing what I could to find out what would be the best for the boy, and not for my own personal gratification.

* * *

To replace Bernie, I had to bring a sophomore up from the reserves, who needed another year before he would be ready.

We opened with Three Rivers on their home court. Three Rivers had a new basketball coach from Indiana. He was anxious to open with the defending state champions. The first half, everything went wrong. Our players seemed tired and completely exhausted. I really couldn't understand it.

I knew we were in good physical condition, but Three Rivers was sweeping us right off the court as we stood around and watched them.

In the second quarter, the Wildcats had us down by 18 points, and at half time it was still a 14 point deficit. The large Wildcat crowd was going wild. They were humiliating the defending state champs.

We were a sorry looking group as we trooped down to the locker room at half time. I wondered, "What can I do to turn this game around, anyway?" I just couldn't understand why we were not playing our game.

"Corless, take your uniform off and take a shower," I angrily shouted at my superstar.

As Corless was taking a shower, I talked to the rest of the squad. I had them shook up.

I knew what they were thinking, "What's the coach doing anyway, pulling the state's best player out of the game?" We had better get going if he's in that kind of mood."

As Corless came out of the shower and dried himself off, I said, "Corless, put your uniform back on now, and get ready to play some ball this half. You ought to be refreshed and feeling great now.

"Now get, all of you, and start running and pressing. I don't want to see any one of you looking tired until after the game."

The Wildcats were blown off the court the last half. They could hardly walk at the end of the game. Our Cardinals looked stronger each minute, winning 57 to 43.

At the same time I was plotting our half time strategy for the second half, the new Wildcat coach was ridiculing the defending state champs. The conversation was relayed to me after the game by a friend who was visiting the Three Rivers locker room at half time.

"So this is a state championship team here in Michigan," he sneered sarcastically. "In Indiana, they would have trouble winning a game all year. If this is the best, then we won't have any trouble winning championships."

However after the game, the coach didn't have anything to say.

* * *

After the Three Rivers game, we opened the league season by defeating Albion. We then lost two in a row to Battle Creek Lakeview and Marshall. It looked like our dynasty had come to an end.

However, we went undefeated the rest of the season winning our fourth consecutive league championship, setting a new record.

After our long winning streak, in order to win the league, we were completely mentally, emotionally, and physically exhausted. With the moving of our big center, Bernie, to Indiana, our small guys not only had to do the running and pressing, but also the rebounding. This year-long rebounding by our small players against taller opponents had taken a lot out of our players.

Our first game in the district was against Three Rivers. Everything seemed to go wrong. Even to the extent that the basketball bounded out of play and onto the lap of my co-worker, Bob, as we sat side by side on the bench.

Immediately, a Wildcat player picked it up out of his lap

and dribbled in and shot the basketball. Neither official saw it and the basket counted.

Later Bob said, "If I only had thrown the ball off my lap and up in the stands, we could have won the championship."

We were behind 40 to 38 with 9 seconds to go when Corless intercepted a pass and dribbled across the center line and to the basket where he made the shot. I knew we were going into overtime, because I knew there were only two seconds left.

The Wildcat guard threw it into Mitchell, a freshman brought up from the reserves for the tournament. Mitchell dribbled the ball back and forth in the front court trying to get through our tight press. He must have taken 12 to 15 seconds trying to get across the center line. When he did, he threw the ball through the net as the gun went off, beating us 42 to 40.

During all this time the two seconds had not run out. I knew immediately what had happened. The tournament timer, who was a Sturgis fan, was so excited about the defending state champions being defeated, he had shut the clock off as Corless scored the tying bucket.

Time was still in after a scored basket but the timer in all of the excitement had made an honest mistake. He then forgot to turn it back on until Mitchell shot the ball.

I was really mad, and was going to contest it. However, I decided if I do, most people will think it's just "sour grapes." It will be a mess with the timer being put on the spot.

I just lowered my head, and walked to the locker room. The Coldwater basketball dynasty had ended. It was a lonely walk for a coach who was bitter in defeat.

Why, I wondered long afterwards, couldn't I remember how much Our Lord had blessed me!

*"Humble yourselves therefore
under the mighty hand of God,
that He may exalt you in due
time"*
1 Peter 5:6

7

BACK TO REALITY AND HUMILITY

"Why don't you plug that whistle with your gum, and let us play some basketball?" I screamed at the game official.

"Sit down and shut up Eby, or I'll throw a technical at you," the official shouted back.

"If you do, it will show your lack of intelligence and knowledge of the game of basketball," I countered.

"Eby why don't you ever read the rules, and then you would know why we are calling so many fouls on your team," the official stated.

I shouted right back, "One thing I know for sure is that you never read the rules, because they don't print the rule book in braille."

"Pat," I turned to my co-worker, "go up in the stands and get me some more ball players. The way these guys are calling 'em, we will need most of our fans to suit up before we finish this game."

* * *

After four years of glorious championships, we were in the midst of some mediocre years. Winning half of our games just wasn't enough for our fans or myself. We had both been spoiled with our previous winning records.

This season's opener with Marshall in our own gym was an indication that this was going to be the worst season of all. I had three excellent ball players coming back from the previous year. Two sharp shooting guards, and an excellent big pivot man.

One of the guards was injured in our last football game and was out for the season. The other guard and the pivot man had been caught stealing pop. I removed them from the squad for the season. This left us without any experienced players.

I brought up some sophomores from the reserve team, and combined them with some inexperienced juniors, and started building for the next year. Naturally, we were playing race horse basketball. The young inexperienced players were just not ready to play this style against varsity competition.

We would have been much better if we had gone to a slower more deliberate pattern of basketball. We could have had closer games, but I knew to get ready for next year, we had to press and race horse.

Our home opener was against an excellent Marshall team who had last year's league leading scorer, Brett, in the starting lineup.

We were being bombed, and losing players like crazy from excessive fouling through close calling by the officials. Only four minutes had gone by in the first quarter, when I lost my big sophomore forward, Rick, with four fouls.

I only dressed ten men for the varsity game which was normal for my coaching. As soon as Rick was waived out of the game, I had Pat call a player down from the stands and dressed him in Rick's uniform.

Noticing how close these same officials were calling fouls in the preliminary game, I listed five more names in the scorebook before the start of the varsity game.

These were players who were not good enough to make the

varsity or the reserve squad, but were still on the eligibility list in case they improved before the end of the season or next year.

Our starting five fouled out shortly after half time intermission. We now had five spectators dressed in our starting five's uniforms.

It wasn't long in the third quarter before we had some of the five spectators playing. During the last five minutes of the game we had all five spectators playing, because by then all our varsity ten had fouled out of the game.

Every time one of our players was kicked out with four fouls, the officials and I would have another row. It seemed like I always lost.

Our five spectator players were really getting mauled. Brett, the league leading scorer, remained in the entire game, scoring 37 points --- the exact number that Marshall creamed us with.

When the gun finally stopped the massacre, I was sick. I strode over to Joe, the Marshall coach, and shook his hand and congratulated him. This was required ethics for the losing coach. I was really tempted to forego it for this one time, but I didn't.

"Congratulations, Joe, you've got a good team," I said without enthusiasm or sincerity.

"Too bad, Floyd," Joe answered. "Perhaps I shouldn't have left Brett in so long, but you know he is a good boy, and I want him to have all the publicity he can get."

"That's all right, Joe," I answered sarcastically. "You can leave Brett in for the rest of the night as far as I am concerned, but I am shutting the lights off and going home!" I turned on my heel and quickly strode into the locker room.

* * *

We continued to get bombed, losing ten games by an average of 37 points each, but the boys were improving each game and becoming much stronger.

Later in the season we traveled to Marshall and gave them

1952 squad learning a new play from Coach Eby.

* * *

the worst beating of the year and on their own court. This was sweet revenge against the Marshall coach who drubbed us in the opener, leaving the league scorer in the entire game. We won only two games all season, but the next year we only lost three.

Joe, the Marshall coach, and I were good friends except for the nights when we played each other. Since retirement we have become close friends as well as brothers in Christ.

* * *

One night we were playing Marshall in their small, outdated gym. The floor of the old gym was so dead that you could barely dribble the basketball on it. Of course the Marshall Redskin players were used to bouncing the ball extra hard.

That season Joe had purchased some new basketballs which turned out to be a bum product, and didn't even bounce decently on a new gym floor. On the Marshall court, it was almost impossible to bounce one hard enough to bring it back up so you could continue the dribble.

I checked the game ball, and realized it was a dead ball. I immediately went to Joe, "Joe this new game ball is a punk and dead ball. I don't want to use it, but I will approve the used ball that you are practicing with. It has a much better bounce than the new one."

"Nothing doing, Eby," Joe answered. "We are going to use the new one, and that's it."

I went to the head official and showed him the game ball. He admitted that the new game ball didn't have the bounce that the practice ball had. The official tried to get Joe and me to agree on one or the other, but to no avail.

Joe told me and the official to follow him into the locker room, which we did. Joe took twelve boxes of new basketballs off a shelf and started unboxing them. As he did, he would throw them at me.

"There you are Eby. If you don't like the one out on the court, try this one, or this one, or this one."

Joe kept throwing new basketballs at me as fast as he could take them out of the boxes. In a few minutes Joe had a dozen new balls bouncing all over the locker room.

I was checking the bounce on every one although it was mighty confusing with them bouncing all over. Each one I checked, even though new, was a pumpkin with a lousy bounce.

I told Joe and the official that I wouldn't approve any of them. I still wanted the used ball that would bounce. Since the official couldn't get us to agree, he decided to go with Joe's new ball.

"Eby," the official notified me, "the rule book states that the home team is to furnish a ball that is in good condition. The rules don't say anything about the bounce, so we will use the new ball."

"Race horse" Basketball produces action.

"How can even a new ball be in good condition, if it won't bounce?" I asked. However, we used the new pumpkin, and our kids really had problems dribbling it.

With two seconds to go, one of Joe's shooters hit a shot clear from the corner to defeat us by one point. I was sick, sick, sick! I went directly to Joe to congratulate him, but he avoided me and ran to his locker room.

I followed him. When I reached the locker room, the team manager, one of their extra large football players, blocked the entrance.

"Coach told me not to let you into the locker room, Mr. Eby," he said.

"Get out of my way, but quick," I shouted, pushing him roughly aside.

I hollered at Joe in the locker room, "Congratulations, Joe, you won a great one."

Douglas 88 and Baysinger 12 survive eligibility scare from practical joker, assistant principal Weaver.

I was still sick and bitter.

I am sure if I had been a mature Christian at the time, I would not have had any trouble with Joe. We are now the best of friends and I respect him greatly, and also love him as a brother in Christ.

* * *

"Don't hand me any of that stuff, Douglas, I don't want any of your lip," I was speaking to one of my star basketball players.

"This has to be your report card. There is your name on it, and also your mother's signature for each previous reporting period."

"I don't care about all of that coach," Douglas answered. "I just don't have all 'D's' and 'E's' on my report card. It just can't be my card, I don't care about the signatures, it is not my card."

The assistant principal, Weaver, had interrupted my practice session to show me two report cards of two of my basketball players, Douglas and Baysinger. Both cards had marks for the last reporting period that made them both ineligible to play basketball.

I couldn't figure it out, as neither had been ineligible before and were good students. I was really mad to think that both of them had "goofed off" during this period and I would have to replace both starters.

Unbeknown to me and the two players, Weaver, who was a practical joker, had faked both report cards. He had both of their original cards traced, including their parents' signatures. Then for the last reporting period, he inserted the failing grades.

After I blew my top, and chewed both of them out in front of the principal and the entire basketball squad, Weaver told me the actual truth.

What a laugh he had.... as well as my basketball squad when they found out how Coach Eby had been tricked. Even Douglas and Baysinger enjoyed my discomfort and embarrassment.

* * *

During a game, I never allowed any of my players to talk with the officials or show any displeasure because of any of the calls of the officials.

I instructed my players that I would stand up for their rights. I didn't want any "belly aching" from them at all. I would take care of the officials.

All the players had to do was to play ball to the best of their ability. I wanted them to concentrate on their play, not on the officiating. I reminded my players that for every foul the official called on them, undoubtedly they had fouled one or more times that were not called.

My players never showed any emotion whatever while on the court playing the game. As a foul was called, immediately they would raise a hand above their heads, and keep a "dead pan" face.

I felt that emotions, released on the court, cut the efficiency of the player, encouraged the opponents, and irritated the officials.

In a game at East Lansing, the official called a questionable foul on Tony, one of my guards. Instead of raising his arm, and showing no emotion, Tony lifted his palms up in a gesture of innocence, with a look of disbelief on his face. He shrugged his shoulders like he couldn't believe the call.

I immediately called time out, and sent Tony to the showers. I replaced him with a substitute which didn't help any, as we lost the game. Losing the game built up my wrath for Tony's actions.

The next week in practice, I informed the squad and Tony that we were going to practice reactions to the calling of questionable fouls by the officials.

I walked up to Tony and cracked him on the shoulder, blew my whistle, and shouted, "Foul on number 22."

Tony immediately raised his arm straight up and briskly walked to the foul line with an unusual "dead pan" face. After a few minutes of such practice and a bruised shoulder on Tony, we had no more emotions shown during the rest of our games.

* * *

As a coach I appreciated hustle and aggressiveness even if a player was short on natural ability. It was most difficult for me to cut a player from the squad if he was a real competitor. One year I had seven decent ball players. Five others were lacking in ability, but were real scrappy players who played with real zest and aggressiveness. I decided not to cut my varsity squad to ten but to keep these five, making a squad of twelve.

I made a special unit out of these five scrappers, and named them the Green Hornets. Their purpose was to enter the game as a unit, and to buzz and sting the opponents by playing race horse basketball with reckless abandon.

With this unit we did not worry about mistakes. The Green Hornets were to race as fast as possible at all times, dive on the floor for the ball, press extra tight, and play the game extra rough under the boards and in the scrambles.

The Green Hornets ran everywhere they went, always as a group. They ran to and from the locker room, sprinted as a unit to the scorer's table to report in, sprinted to the foul lines when lining up for a free throw; sprinted to their positions for jump balls, and sprinted to the bench when leaving the game. All five went everywhere at the same time.

The purpose of this unit was to inspire the rest of our varsity squad to hustle and race, to discourage and confuse our opponents, to tire the opponents and the officials, and to create a tempo in the game that was to our advantage when the starters came back into the game.

The Hornets were also an enthusiastic group who encouraged each other as well as the rest of our varsity.

The crowd loved the Hornets, and would give them a real ovation as they sprinted into the game as a unit, and then sprinted back to the bench as they were relieved. Even more important, the Hornets received the advantage of playing varsity athletics instead of being cut.

* * *

Each pre-season, after I had selected my varsity squad and before the first game, I would call a meeting of all the players and their parents. We would have an evening potluck.

After eating I would send the varsity squad down to the gym to play volleyball while I talked to their parents as a group.

During this meeting I would go over all my rules with the parents, giving them an opportunity to ask questions, and to understand the reasons for such rules. This was a great time for building a solid understanding between the coach and the parents of my players.

I instructed them on many matters. "You and I have a

common goal. The building of your son into an outstanding citizen. We both have the welfare of your son foremost in our relationship with him. We are both interested in his health, grades, conduct, and progress --- mentally, emotionally, socially, and physically.

"I never will criticize you to your son, and I will never criticize your son to you or to anyone else. I will deal directly with him in our squad meetings, and privately. I am asking for your cooperation to help me train your son, so he will be a son that you will always be proud of.

"You may criticize me as a coach or as an individual all you want to each other, to your neighbors, and friends. But please do not criticize me to your boy or in front of your son.

"In fact, if I find out that you are criticizing me to or in front of your boy, I will cut your son from the squad. You see as you criticize me to your son, you are causing him to lose faith in me as a coach.

"Once he loses faith in me as a coach, I can no longer use him. Because I can no longer have any influence with him. He will no longer produce to the best of his ability, and will no longer be any use to our varsity squad. You really don't hurt me as you criticize me to your son, you only hurt the one you love the most, your son.

"I will still be coach, but your son has lost his privilege to play varsity basketball. He now will be more available to get into trouble with drugs, alcohol, and the law. I also love your son and want only the best for him that will help him have a happy, fruitful life."

I praise God that nearly all the parents cooperated with the rules and guidelines.

* * *

"Fellows, I called this meeting to remind you that as you take your senior trip to Washington, D.C., you will be expected to obey all the training rules while you are on the trip if you expect to play spring sports when you come back," I said.

"You helped to set up these training rules, and there will be no exceptions. All of you have signed up to play either baseball, track, or golf this spring. Therefore your training rules will extend to the senior trip. Goodbye, good luck, have a good time, but stay in training."

I was talking to our senior athletes just before they took off to Washington, D.C. with the rest of the senior class for a week in the Nation's Capitol. I really didn't worry about this group of seniors. For four years this same group had stayed in training the year around to play sports at Coldwater High School. They prided themselves on being the best trained squad in our league.

The seniors arrived back from Washington, D.C. as school commenced after spring vacation. The first day that school was in session, I knew something was wrong. I heard no rumors about what had happened on the senior trip, but I knew something had.

As I met senior athletes in the hall and gave them my usual "Hi, John," they would answer, "Hi, Coach."

However, they did not look at me, or would turn the other way, and this was not normal.

As I supervised the study hall, I could feel students staring at me. As I turned to look, I could see a girl or boy student staring at me with fear on his or her face.

I couldn't wait any longer. I called Gordon, my basketball co-captain, into my office. Gordon was an excellent kid, and a good athlete.

"Sit down, Gordon, I want to talk to you," I began. "Why did you break training rules on the Washington trip?" I threw the bomb at him. I really didn't know that he had but I knew he would tell the truth.

Gordon came right back, "I guess I did, because I didn't want to play baseball as bad as I did football and basketball. I have no excuses, and I deserve not to be able to play. I knew better. I am just sorry if I let the baseball team down."

I sent Gordon back to class. From then on, one after another came to my office to report their violation of training rules on spring vacation. No one reported anyone except himself. Even underclassmen athletes came forth to report their own violations.

I was really surprised and disappointed, because I had so much faith in my senior athletes. However, I felt real proud of each one of them also, as they came in on their own, and confessed their wrong doing. I just knew that they had learned a valuable lesson and would be good citizens of our community and country.

I called a varsity club meeting. I asked all those that felt they no longer qualified to be a varsity club member to please dismiss themselves from the meeting. All those who had reported themselves walked out plus several other underclassmen.

I asked the rest of the club what they thought ought to be done. The rest of the club was unanimous in thinking that all violators should be punished, even though many of the club members were close friends of the violators.

Our entire coaching staff came to me to discuss this current problem. All coaches felt that because most of these violators had been in strict training for four years, and had never before broken the rules, that we should set up a program to help those who wanted to come back on the spring sport teams.

The coaches decided that the violators could practice with the squads. They would have a special 8:00 p.m. training curfew every night during the week for four weeks, and would miss the first two contests that were played.

All violators agreed wholeheartedly to take their punishment like a man, and work themselves back onto the squads. The matter seemed to be settled satisfactorily from all points of view.

However, there was one unsatisfied group that I hadn't planned on. The parents of the violators. Although none of them came to me personally, rumors of their feelings soon became known to me. I called a meeting of all of the parents of all the violators.

The large classroom was crowded with parents, coaches, the principal, and superintendent. No students or athletes had been invited and none were present.

I could feel dynamite in this meeting. I knew the wrong thing said by anyone would cause a real explosion, and someone, and perhaps many, were going to get hurt. Feelings were running high, and this meeting could cause hard feelings that would last for a lifetime.

I just knew that I had to take complete charge of the meeting, and I did.

I explained that the purpose of the meeting was to notify personally the parents about training rule violations of their sons, and the action that had been taken by the coaching staff. I then offered to entertain any question which dealt with the facts of the violations or the program.

One father spoke up, "Coach, we have no argument with your high standards of conduct for our sons. Certainly, your program has really helped the youth of our community. But there is one thing that we do not understand and we do dislike greatly. That is having the team members tell on one another. All our lives we have taught our sons not to be a tattle tale, and your program encourages it."

I answered, "Our varsity club program on training rules calls for self enforcement. The team members in the varsity club set up and agree to follow the program. If your son is off the squad because of training violations, it is because he broke the rules that he helped set up and agreed to abide with.

"If a team member knows that his teammate is breaking training, he goes to this teammate and encourages him to turn himself in. The reason for this is that all team members believe it is wrong for one boy to be off the squad for breaking training and to allow another one to get by with it.

"Sir," I asked the father, "if you saw someone robbing the bank and you knew who it was, would you report the person to the police or not?"

"Sure I would," he answered, "but that is important."

"That is where you and I disagree," I countered. "How many filling stations have not been robbed in this community because of our high standards and training maintained by our high school athletes?"

"You see, sir, you and I don't really disagree except on where to draw the line. You want to wait until it turns into big-time robbery or even homicide. We feel wrong is wrong and should be dealt with while it is still curable."

Another parent bitterly shouted out, "Eby, you sure have a bunch of Mickey Mouse rules for my son to follow to get back on the team. Whoever heard of an 8:00 p.m. curfew every night for an eighteen year old boy? I expected my boy to sow some wild oats on the trip, and for you to hold it against him is strictly small time stuff."

I interrupted him, "I have heard all I want to hear from you. I could care less why you sent your son to Washington. However, the trip was organized to give your son an experience with the historical heritage of this country, and to build pride for this country. If you sent him there to booze it up, you could have kept him at home to do that in your own home.

"Before I close this meeting," I continued firmly, "I want everyone of you to know that I am proud of every one of your sons. Each one reported himself, and told me personally that he was wrong and was willing to accept any punishment we decided on. I believe this shows results of excellent training.

"I know our country will be in good hands with young citizens like your sons. I am sure if your sons had their way about it, none of you would have been in this meeting. They were willing to work it out on their own. They know the difference between right and wrong, and I praise God for them. The meeting is now dismissed as no further discussion is necessary."

That ended the meeting and the problem.

I am proud of the athletes I have coached over the years. To the best of my knowledge, not one I personally coached ever ended up or spent time in jail. Certainly it wasn't of my doing, but I praise God for it.

I am thankful for the boys' willingness to cooperate with training and conduct guidelines.

Gordon, the first one to confess, is now a wonderful

Christian man with a Christian family. He is active in his
Church and in other Christian organizations. Others are
ministers, and most all of them are outstanding citizens.

Left to right: Coach Bob Livermore, Coach "Sunny" Bauer, Coach
Floyd Eby. Eby and Livermore were co-workers. "Sunny" Bauer was
long time Coldwater coach before Coach Eby. Picture was taken
during Coldwater-Marshall Basketball game in 1949 in Old National
Guard Armory.

"These things I have spoken unto you, that in me ye might have peace. In the world ye shall have tribulation; but be of good cheer; I have overcome the world."
John 16:33

8

TRIALS, TRIBULATIONS, AND THE BLESSINGS   OF A COACH

"You know that's an illegal screen. The block is being set too close to my defensive player. You know it's illegal and wrong. Why do you insist on doing it?" I shouted at Dave, the opposing coach.

"Baloney, baloney," he shouted back.

"You quit your swearing Dave," I screamed. That is the closest I ever heard Dave come to swearing. Dave is a real believer.

We were playing our arch rivals at Sturgis. Dave, the Sturgis basketball coach, was one of my closest coaching friends as well as my brother in Christ. We never had any disagreements except during a game. Then we agreed on very little. Our full court zone press had caused our opponents troubles for many years, but in this game Dave was beating it.

He would throw the ball to his best dribbling guard in our front court. As he tried to dribble forward, my defensive player would cut him off. Dave was stationing one of his players right in back of my player who couldn't see him. As the dribbler would start around my player, my player would move to the side and backwards to go with him.

When this happened the teammate of the dribbler would fall on his back to the floor like my man had pushed him. The rule book called for a three foot clearance, so my defensive player would have the opportunity to avoid the collision upon seeing this block.

Dave, naturally, claimed that his player was allowing the necessary three foot clearance.

As the Sturgis player fell to the floor, I rushed out onto the court quickly followed by Dave and one of the officials.

I shouted at both of them, "You ought to give number twenty-two an 'Oscar' for his acting ability --- not a free throw for an illegal 'pick'."

Two thousand Sturgis fans started booing me, loud and nasty.

I never was very popular with the Sturgis fans. The booing only made me more angry. I took my rule book out of my coat pocket, and tried to show the applicable rule to the official and Dave. This only made the booing more intense.

As usual I lost the argument, and it seemed to me that number twenty-two was shooting free throws all night for his acting ability on that illegal pick.

John Bailey, one of the game officials, had the nickname of "Chokie." During the first half, every Sturgis player who made a basket would slap the ball out of bounds after it cleared the net.

"Chokie," I screamed at the official, "that's a technical foul and I want it called."

The next time a Sturgis player slapped the ball after he made a basket, Chokie called a technical foul and we shot a free throw.

The Sturgis players were in such a habit that they continued to do it unintentionally. After six Sturgis baskets, we shot six free throws. I thought that this might make up for some of the free throws that number twenty-two was

Collisions are difficult to avoid in race horse basketball.

getting for his acting ability.

Dave was really uptight about the technicals called on his players.

"Chokie, this is entirely unintentional and a matter of habit and you should disregard it," he pleaded.

"That makes no difference, Chokie," I yelled.

"The rule book states clearly that we have the right to that ball as soon as it goes through the net, and that it is a technical foul for the opposing team to take that right away from us."

This conversation took place right at the end of the first half just before we went to the locker rooms for our halftime break.

During the second half the Sturgis players continued to habitually slap the ball out of bounds after each basket, but Chokie quit calling the technicals.

"So they got to you at halftime, eh, Chokie," I chided. After each violation I reminded him of his lack of intestinal fortitude in giving in to the Sturgis pressure.

However, it all came to a screeching halt when I yelled at him once again, "Chokie, don't you let them do that once more. I am not going to take it any longer. This nonsense has got to stop - and right now."

It did, as he called a technical foul on me, and I shut up.

My co-worker, Pat, said I took off my suit coat and threw it at him, but I didn't realize it. We lost the game by a couple of points.

After the game, Chokie came up to me. "Floyd, the only reason I called that technical on you, was because you shouted and called me by my first name."

"That's a lie," I said.

"In the registration bulletin your name is John Bailey, and I shouted out 'Chokie.' How do you know I wasn't talking to one of my players by that nickname?" I left for the locker room.

However, after the game, Dave and I were once again close friends, and our relationship with Jesus was once again where it should be.

* * *

Basketball officials were always irritating to me. I realize I was prejudiced. Never once did I feel that I ever got a break in the officiating. Of course, that was impossible to never receive a break during the many years I coached basketball. I knew I had to be looking at the calls with prejudiced eyes.

I loved the basketball officials before and after the game. However, the striped black and white shirts of the officials during the game drew the same response from me as waving a red flag draws from a bull. I guessed I felt the officials were always against me and my style of ball.

John was a tall, handsome basketball official. The first time he officiated for Coldwater, I tried baiting him. "John, you sure missed that one, didn't you?"

John just looked at me and gave me a big smile and didn't say a word. Every time I shouted at him, he would just smile and not say a word. I finally gave up and quit trying to bait him.

From then on I just loved his officiating. The players loved him also because he would never get upset. We hired him every chance we got.

John used a Biblical guideline, "A slow or no answer turneth away wrath."

* * *

We were playing at Albion during my last year of coaching, and Jim was one of the officials. Jim was a very particular and technical person, and therefore he generally irritated me.

After he had called a foul on one of my players down at the other end of the floor and as the players and officials walked up to the other foul line near me, I casually remarked, "You sure haven't improved much over the summer have you, Jim?"

"Floyd," he said, "you know I'm a real 'homer' over here at Albion. I always call 'em in their favor."

THE BLESSINGS OF A COACH/129

He continued to josh me. "You know Floyd my real trouble is that I really need glasses."

I immediately took off my glasses, and held them out to him. "Here, Jim. You can borrow mine if it will help."

That did it. Jim gave the technical foul sign and shouted "That's a technical on you, Eby."

I sat down and shut up. After both the technical and personal foul had been shot, a timeout was called by Albion.

Jim sauntered over to my bench. "Floyd, do you want to know why I called that technical on you?"

"Get away from me, Jim, just get away from me," I answered. "I don't want to have anything to do with you. That was a cheap shot. Just leave me alone."

"No, Floyd, I want you to really know why I called that technical," he continued. "I only need single focals and you

Officials are a necessary part of the game.

offered me your bifocals."

Pat, my co-worker, really told Jim off at halftime. But I never said another word.

In spite of many incidents like these with many different officials during many games, all of the officials I knew were fine men and actually good friends of mine -- except during the games.

* * *

"Listen, Eby. If it's the last thing I ever do, I am going to get you fired," he angrily shouted over the phone.

"Thank you Mr. Crull," I answered softly. "Perhaps you can be a real help to me. I tried to resign three years ago and the School Board and administration wouldn't let me. Perhaps, with your influence, you can help me secure what I want."

He hung up. The man at the other end of the line was Pete Crull, the father of one of our star football players I had terminated from the squad for breaking training rules.

Ted was a good kid and an excellent football player and wrestler. However, after our last varsity game, Ted had gone out with some of his friends and had been coaxed into drinking a beer. I had heard a rumor about it, so I called Ted into my office.

I had learned a line of questioning that never failed to bring a confession of truth. As I questioned Ted, I knew he was really squirming both inside and out, indicating to me that he was really guilty.

However, Ted didn't want to lose what he liked the most --- playing varsity football. He hedged continually, refusing to admit his guilt. He then broke down and told the truth.

It never failed when one of my athletes would finally admit their guilt that even though they were losing the one thing they treasured the most, athletics, a look of genuine relief would appear on their faces. I always thought of the Bible verse, *John 8:32 "And ye shall know the truth, and the truth shall make you free."*

THE BLESSINGS OF A COACH/131

"Ted, you know what this means. You are through playing football this season," I told him.

"Yes, Coach," Ted answered. "I deserve my punishment. It was my fault."

"Well, Ted, let's get into my car and I will take you home. You know we are going to have to tell your father."

"Please, Coach," he implored. "Don't you go with me. I want to tell dad by myself. He's going to be awful mad. I don't want you around."

"You sure you will go straight home and tell your dad now?" I asked. Ted promised he would.

Ted didn't go home.

Instead he ran away from home by hitchhiking to South Bend, Indiana. I didn't know this until later that night when Mr. Crull called me after he found out from one of Ted's friends what had happened.

"Eby, if anything happens to my boy, wherever he is, I am going to hold you personally responsible. And I will sue you," Mr. Crull said.

"Mr. Crull," I said, "I offered to bring your boy home and tell you about the incident, but Ted didn't want it that way.

"Don't try to make me responsible just because your relationship with your son is in such a sorry state that he would rather run away from home rather than bring a problem to his dad when he needs help."

"I will tell you one thing, Eby, you will never have a winning basketball team this winter, because I am going to check on all your basketball players. If any one of them is breaking training, I am going to find out. And I will make you kick each one off the squad," he threatened.

"Mr. Crull, you bring me the evidence. I will eliminate them from basketball. You won't have to make me do it," I answered, and then hung up.

I told my basketball squad that winter that I had some special help in enforcing training rules. A certain citizen was going to follow them around all winter. If anyone broke any training rules, I would be notified. We had excellent training all winter.

STATE CHAMPS   Seated left to right: Dr. Olmstead, Livermore, Sowles, Eby, Cox, Grigg.   Standing left to right: Judge Stansell, Rosenberg, Corless, Rhodes, Engle, Cooper, Simmons, Clark, McConnell, Hogoboom, Weeks, Fry and Porter.

* * *

Eric, one of our local businessmen was an avid sports fan. He was a booster of our high school athletic teams, but he also considered himself a self-appointed assistant coach. All of our coaches heard from Eric regularly, either in person or by letter, with information about how we could improve our coaching and the team.

As I was giving last minute instructions to my team near our bench in Jenison Field House at Michigan State University, someone tapped me on the shoulder. When I turned around Eric immediately handed me an envelope and left. I stuck it in my coat pocket, and then completed my instructions.

The starting five trotted out to the center jump to start the state championship game with River Rouge High School. After winning the game for the state championship, and spending a great night in afterglow, my co-worker, Bob, and I got up early to take the team to church services before we started back to Coldwater.

As I put on my coat to go to breakfast, I located the envelope Eric had given me the night before. I opened it and found Eric's own personal scouting report of River Rouge with complete instructions on how to beat them. Although I did not see Eric's scouting report until the morning after the game, I am sure Eric felt responsible for our first state championship.

About two years later I started receiving letters from Eric. I opened the first one, and as I commenced to read it I soon found it very derogatory about my coaching. I read the first paragraph only, placed it back into the envelope and filed it in my bottom desk drawer. I continued to receive letters from him, but I didn't open them. I filed them in the same desk drawer.

After several weeks I thought perhaps Eric actually felt his letters to me were the real reason for the improvement of the team. I decided to write Eric a letter and set him straight.

"Dear Eric," I wrote. "I am writing to you to let you know that I have not been reading the letters you have been sending me. In fact, after reading the first paragraph of the first letter, and finding it critical of my coaching, I have refused to even open the other letters. All letters are now filed in my bottom desk drawer, still sealed as delivered.

"I am telling you this, Eric, so you will no longer waste your valuable time telling me how to coach. I do not, and will not come down to your company and tell you how to conduct your business. I am not going to have any fan tell me how to coach my basketball team.

"I am sure your record as a successful businessman indicates that you know what you are doing. My record as a coach also indicates that I have been properly trained, and that I know what I am doing. I suggest you stick to what you are trained to do and leave the coaching up to me."

> Sincerely yours,
> Coach Floyd Eby

I did not receive any more letters from Eric.

* * *

"Coach Eby, we have to have the gym right now to decorate for the prom," Cindy explained. Cindy and Pat, two of our outstanding junior girls, were asking me to dismiss basketball practice when I had just started. It was

3:30 p.m. and the boys were just warming up. I knew the prom was a great event in the life of our junior and senior students, and I certainly was in favor of the event.

However, the committee members had not told me they needed the gym right after school for decorating. If I had been told, I would have held basketball practice at 6:00 in the morning in order to accommodate the students and sponsors. Since I hadn't, I was now in a position of badly needing a practice to ready the team for the next game.

"Girls," I said, "I am sorry but I need to practice. You can have the gym at 5:00. We will quit early."

"That will not give us enough time," Cindy exploded. "We hardly have enough time now, because we all have to go home and get ready."

"I am sorry girls," I repeated. "I will be through at 5:00." I walked back to practice.

About five minutes later, Paul, our principal, came in the gym and called me off to the side.

"I am sorry Coach that the committee didn't reserve the gym for decorations, but despite the mistake, they have to have it --- now. You will have to call off practice."

"Paul," I answered, "they can have it at 5:00." I went back to practice.

Ten minutes later, our superintendent, Mr. Craig, showed up. He also called me off to the side. Mr. Craig and Paul, the principal, were wonderful men and I dearly loved and respected both of them.

"Coach Eby," Mr. Craig spoke in his soft and lovable voice, "I am very sorry about this misunderstanding, but the decorating committee must have the gym now."

"Mr. Craig," I interrupted, "they can have the gym at 5:00."

Once again I went back to practice.

I knew there might be a chance I could be fired because of my refusal to do as my superiors ordered. However, I thought it was wrong to punish my team by sending them into the next game unprepared. The gym was my classroom. I never used any other teachers' classroom without their permission.

I dismissed practice sharply at 5:00 and sent the boys upstairs for showers. I also went up to shower and dress. The decorating committee went to work in the gym which by now was filled with hostility. As the players dressed and then came down through the gym, unknown to me, they started giving the girls a bad time.

"I guess you know who runs the school now, don't you girls?

"You gals have had your way around this school long enough. Even the principal and superintendent couldn't swing it for you this time. I guess you know now you will have to go to Coach Eby."

This made the girls angrier by the minute.

As I came downstairs and stepped into the gym, I could feel the intense feelings and even hatred that the situation and the boys had stirred up.

When I walked across the gym, there was dead silence. If looks would kill, I would have died right there. I didn't say a word. I just started helping them decorate. I worked with them for thirty minutes in a very hostile atmosphere with no communications.

Finally Cindy broke the silence. "Coach, what really made us mad were those brats you have on the basketball team. They were just irritating with their comments. But we are sorry for our actions. We should have told you sooner."

I also apologized for being so stubborn and for the actions of my players.

We finished up the decorating in a friendly fashion, and we had a great prom that night.

As Jesus said in *James 1:19* *"Wherefore, my beloved brethren, let every man be swift to hear, slow to speak, slow to wrath."*

Oh, Lord, why do I reverse your guidelines for my life. Why is it that I don't want to listen. I am so quick to speak, and so fast to become angry. Please help me, Lord, to live a life pleasing to you!

* * *

I was a great believer in experimenting with new rules, policies, procedures, and ideas. If the new ones worked, I would incorporate them into my coaching career. If not, I would discard them.

One year I instituted a rule concerning the relationship between my basketball players and their girl friends. If we lost a ball game, the players were not to see their girl friends until the next day. The players were to go directly home with their parents or by themselves.

This new rule immediately created a lot of static around the school, especially among the girl friends. Although the players did not seem to be so concerned, their girl friends and other students and adults thought the new rule was strictly "Mickey Mouse."

I guess God had made me quite stubborn, because I would never consider giving in to pressure. I called a meeting of all the players' girl friends, and met with them by myself.

"Girls, I called this meeting to let you know first hand that I could care less how you feel about the new rule," I said. "The rule is here to stay for the entire season. If you want your boyfriend to remain on the team, then you will help him not to violate the rule. You can see your boyfriend after each and every game this entire season if we win every game. This meeting is now dismissed."

The girls left the room with their heads down. They were disappointed and angry but they knew better than to say anything. Whenever I met students in the hall, I would smile and nod my head, and sometimes would say "Hi" calling them by name. The students would always acknowledge my greeting.

Now, some of the girl friends would answer my greeting with a snub, turning their heads the other way.

I thought to myself, "Who do those young smart alecs think they are anyway?"

I felt like snubbing them back. Then I realized that the Bible would have me treat them extra nice, which I did. In a few days all of the girl friends were acknowledging my greetings once again.

We won our first five games, and every one was happy including the girl friends. Our sixth game was at Marshall High School. Our boys played an excellent game except for our shooting. The ball would not fall through the net for us. We lost by one point.

The players and I both were dejected over our first loss, especially after playing a good floor game. As I walked into the locker room where the players were hurriedly showering and dressing in preparation for our bus ride back to Coldwater, I almost relented.

Thinking to myself, "Eby, the boys played an excellent game tonight. All of them really hustled and put out. It wasn't their fault that the shots would not fall. We worked the ball good and had excellent shots. I really should do away with that rule for tonight and let them see their girl friends as soon as we arrive in Coldwater.

"What's the matter Eby, are you getting soft? You know that once you set a rule and promise to use it for the entire season, there is no way that you can change it," I told myself.

"Now hear this fellows," I announced to the players. "If any of you want to see your girl friends when we arrive home tonight, you can turn your uniform in now as you no longer will be on this team."

That ended that. We only lost three games all year!

* * *

Jake was a special basketball player, but was handicapped with a lousy disposition and a bad temper. His teammates liked him and nicknamed him "Slick." Jake was really slick around that offensive basket.

He couldn't shoot out court very well, but he was an excellent driver. He could practically always shake his defensive player with his special moves, and drive for a "dog" shot. Jake, overall, was probably our most valuable player.

My stubbornness and Jake's bad temper occasionally brought on a confrontation between us. I would never tolerate a display of emotion during either a practice or a game. I insisted that every player control his emotions toward the officials, coaches, teammates, and opposing players. I always maintained that I would protect their rights. All the players had to do was play the game to the best of their abilities.

As we were scrimmaging against Bronson High School one day, Jake was fouled badly by a Bronson player. He reacted by pushing the player back.

Coldwater straining to secure a jump ball tip from the Lakeview Spartan Giants.

"Jake, knock that off," I shouted.

You could tell by looking at Jake's eyes that he was really seething for being reprimanded before the other players.

A short time later, Jake and a Bronson player dove for a loose ball and sharply collided. As they got up off the floor for a jump ball, Jake once again pushed the Bronson player.

Once again I yelled. "Jake, either you stop this nonsense and play the game the way I insist, or you get out and stay out. Do you understand?"

Jake mumbled something and took off like a streak for the locker room. After practice, he was nowhere to be found. It looked like I had lost my star player for good, and Jake had given up the opportunity to play basketball his last season.

I was so disgusted I didn't really care that much. Several hours later some of my players came to me. They wanted "Slick" back on the team, and they wanted to know if I would at least talk with him. I agreed.

Jack and I sat down by ourselves and worked things out. We did not have any more serious confrontations that year, but I always felt that Jake disliked me. This bothered me because I felt I had failed in my relationship with my athletes if they didn't really like me.

After graduation, Jake moved to a distant community. Many years later, he came back to Coldwater for a short visit, and he came to visit me. He told me how he felt I had influenced his life for good. I told Jake that I was so proud to see that he had become such an outstanding citizen with such a good job.

I praise God that He has been able to use me in some little way in spite of my stubbornness and ability to make so many mistakes.

* * *

Our head football Coach, Hugh, was readying his team for our opening football game. Barry, a transfer from Indiana had moved into our area over the summer. Barry was an excellent quarterback, just the player Hugh needed to have a championship team. We had already drubbed a nearby school in our pre-season scrimmage with Barry at the helm.

As Athletic Director, I sent to Barry's former Indiana High School for a transcript of credits. This was required by our State Athletic Association. After failing to receive any correspondence from his former school, I called Barry into my office. My time limit was up to send out an eligibility list to the school for our opening game.

"Barry," I told him, "I can't get any answer from your former school. I need some answers to verify your eligibility."

"What do you need to know?" Barry asked.

"For one thing," I said, "I need to know your age."

"That's easy, Coach. I am eighteen."

"That's too easy, Barry. I need some proof."

"I have a birth certificate in my billfold," he volunteered. He handed it to me and I told him to go back to football practice.

I looked the birth certificate over, and everything seemed to be in order. Barry was obviously eighteen, which would allow him to play his senior year.

I was just ready to file it, when I took another close look at the date of birth. It just didn't look right, and I had the feeling that it might have been tampered with. I really had been somewhat suspicious because I knew that Indiana high schools were not in the habit of losing excellent athletes like Barry to other schools.

I decided to call the court house in the town in Ohio where Barry was born. I discovered why Barry had transferred to Coldwater High. He was now nineteen years old and too old to play high school athletics in either Indiana or Michigan. I presumed that the Indiana school was trying to do Barry a favor by not answering my correspondence.

I went immediately to the practice field, and called Hugh off to one side to give him the bad news.

"Hugh, Barry is too old to play athletics and is ineligible to play sports at Coldwater High this year."

What a blow to our hard working Christian Coach! Hugh

looked as though he had lost his last friend.

* * *

As head golf coach one spring, I was giving instructions to the squad. "Fellows, one thing I won't tolerate is lying about your scores. I don't care how bad they are, either in practice or in matches, but I cannot stand cheating by miscounting.

"We must base our lives on truth. If we lie about our scores, the only way we can improve our golf is by improving our lying. The Bible states that the truth will set us free. One way we can have a real outstanding life is by basing all our actions on truth!"

Bill was an excellent kid, but a lousy golfer. One night in practice I was playing in a foursome with Bill and two other players. After putting out on the number one green, I asked each player his score on the hole.

Bill had encountered all kinds of trouble on Number One including a sand trap partially hidden by a bunker. In my own mind, Bill had taken eleven strokes by the time he had made his last putt into the hole.

"What was your score Bill?" I asked.

"Twelve," Bill answered.

"Bill, I corrected him, you only had eleven. Your second shot landed in the sand trap. You took four shots to get out of the trap, two more to get on the green, and three putts for an eleven. Isn't that right, Bill?"

"You're right, Coach," Bill replied. "I added an extra stroke, because I didn't want anyone to think I cheated in the sand trap."

Bill was that honest. You would just know that Bill is one of our outstanding citizens and businessman in our local community. I certainly would trust Bill with all things.

* * *

We were playing Sturgis in baseball in Coldwater. Not only was Sturgis our most intense rival, but Bob, the Sturgis baseball coach, was one of the best coaches in the state. Very seldom would Bob's team lose.

We were tied 9 to 9 and were in extra innings. I had used all my substitutes in trying to upset favored Sturgis. Most of the boys on the bench who had not yet been in the game, could hardly carry a bat or ball much less hit or field.

Jack, my regular first baseman, was an excellent fielder, but he just couldn't hit. Jack was almost an automatic out for the opposing team.

We were in the last half of the tenth inning with two out and the bases empty with Jack the next batter. The outlook was really bleak, because I knew we had little chance of holding powerful Sturgis another inning.

Jack picked up his bat and instead of walking up to the batter's box he walked over to me at the bench. "Coach," he asked, "Don't you have a pinch hitter for me? You know I can't hit that ball. Put a pinch hitter in for me Coach, and give the team a chance."

"I sure would Jack if I had anyone, but I am fresh out. Go up there and take your three swings, and we will go to the eleventh inning."

On the first pitch, Jack swung and knocked the ball over the well house in left field for a home run. We won the game 10 to 9. It proved that miracles still happen, and that we can win even with lousy coaching.

* * *

Gene was only 5 foot 5 inches tall, but an excellent all-star player in football, basketball, baseball, and track. He was a real competitor who never complained or made excuses.

In fact, I had to watch him carefully because he would hide his injuries and sicknesses and try to play over them. He was such a competitor that he played well in spite of injuries and sickness.

Gene was the only member of our track team to qualify for the state finals. He and I drove to the state finals in my car. He obviously was sick. He was coughing and blowing his

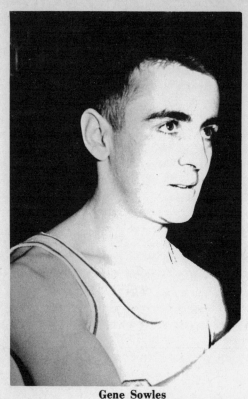

Gene Sowles
No Excuses - just determination.

nose almost continuously. He looked very pale and weak.

"How do you feel, Gene?" I asked.

"Good, Coach," he answered.

"I am not so sure I should let you run," I said. "You're obviously sick."

"Coach, I really feel OK," he pleaded. "This is just a little cold. I just have to run in the finals today."

"You realize, Gene, that you will be running against the best runners in the State. Many of their times are much better than your best time this season. It doesn't make sense to go into a race in poor physical condition when the competition demands your very best."

"I know Coach, but I want to compete and this is my last year," he stated. I reluctantly consented to let him enter the race.

The half mile run started out of the chute at the Michigan State track. No lanes were staggered for the curve. A mob of entries gathered with the officials, and tickets were drawn to determine which lane you drew.

With at least 30 contestants of the best runners in the State, it was necessary to have several contestants in each lane with one after another lined up in each lane. Unfortunately, Gene drew the sixth lane and was placed behind several others in his lane.

All season long, Gene ran the same type of race. He had to get out front and stay there to win. The bigger guys all had a "kick" at the end, and would generally pass the smaller runners with an explosive sprint at the very end.

Gene never had this super sprint at the end of the half mile. He had to depend on a large lead to keep him in front at the finish line.

"Gene," I instructed him, "you are going to have to sprint out of that chute, and get a lead before you reach the first curve. This is a mess with you in your starting position, but somehow you are going to have to get ahead of them before that first curve."

Gene didn't say anything. He looked the same as he did before all other contests he played ... very determined.

At the crack of the starter's gun, thirty contestants shot out of that chute all with the same idea, to get the lead before they reached the first curve. What a thundering stampede. As they rounded the first curve, Gene was 12th. On the back stretch, Gene picked his way through the crowd. He was 8th as they went around the second curve.

On the next stretch, Gene passed three more runners, and was running 5th as they ran the last curve. I thought to myself, if he can hold this position, he will place fifth and receive a state medal. However, those big guys will exercise their kick coming off that curve and they'll leave Gene behind on the final stretch to the finish line. I thought Gene might be lucky to end up 12th.

Coming off the last curve, for the first time in his career, Gene used a "kick" of his own and passed the other four runners like they had quit. He won the State half mile going away.

Praise God for determination and no excuses. I would pray that I would have the same determination, and persistence in serving my Lord, and eliminate all my excuses, as Gene did in winning the half mile race.

* * *

Johnny, the head football coach at Three Rivers, and I were rooming together at Coaching School at Mt. Pleasant. Our two schools, Coldwater and Three Rivers, were meeting head-on this coming fall in the opening football game of the season. Naturally, we spent much of our time discussing that opening game. Johnny was an excellent coach who later coached at Notre Dame, Kentucky, and in the Pros.

"Ebe," Johnny warned me, "I am going to have my nose guard belt your center every time he snaps the ball. My nose guard is the strongest and meanest player I have. He will have your center so worked over that he will be snapping that ball over the head of your tailback and punter. I can hardly wait to see that."

"Johnny," I answered, "Mickey is not near as fragile as he appears. I will have him ready to take on anything that your nose guard can dish out. At Coldwater we build players with character, and your nose guard will not scare my center one bit."

Mickey, my center, was a tall, slender, fragile looking kid. His legs were real spindly, especially around the ankles. His arms were small and skinny, and he didn't look like a football player, certainly not a center. However, Mickey was an excellent kid, a good football, basketball, and baseball player with much determination and courage. He was also a real worker and a competitor.

During practice the week before the Three Rivers game, I personally worked with Mickey a short time each night. As he would snap the ball back to the punter, I would really belt him and knock him on his back. I knew that Johnny's nose guard would be unable to dish out more punishment than I could.

Each night I spent time belting Mickey as he practiced centering to our punter, to try to unnerve him. Mickey never waivered, but always centered the ball perfectly.

The night before the game, I decided that Mickey had had enough and I would not take time to practice with him. Then I changed my mind and decided to keep it fresh in his mind by just trying three snaps.

On the very first snap, as I tried to push through Mickey, his arm was broken.

He couldn't play the rest of the season. I felt bad because Mickey was such a good kid, and he wanted to play his senior year. But he never complained.

To make matters worse, Johnny's nose guard never touched my substitute center all night. Instead, he played the gap. Oh, how I wish I had never listened to that crazy Johnny.

However, I still feel good to see what an outstanding citizen Mickey is today. His determination and courage are being used fully in our Country in the responsible position he has today.

*"Wherefore, my beloved brethren,
let every man be swift to hear,
slow to speak, slow to wrath;
For the wrath of man worketh not
the righteousness of God."*
James 1:19-20

9

A NEW FOOTBALL REGIME

"That's the last we will see of you, Eby."

"You will get fired for sure now, Eby."

"What a dumb coach you are, Eby."

"It's about time Coldwater got rid of you anyway, Eby."

"We sure have had enough of you, Eby."

"Bum, bum, bum, bum, Eby."

"It serves you right, Eby. You are getting just what you deserved."

We had just lost our last football game of the season at Sturgis. As my football squad and I were making our way to the team bus to drive to the locker room to shower, forty or fifty Sturgis fans, both adults and students, were really giving me the once over.

Several of my own players pleaded with me. "Coach, we'll punch 'em in the nose if you'll let us."

"Never mind, fellows," I said. "They are just out of their minds. Get into the bus right now."

I was sick and bitter over the loss. We had an 85 yard touchdown play called back for a penalty. My excited place kicker, an exchange student from Germany, went into the game to kick two extra points without his helmet on, and Sturgis protested each one.

However, the officials allowed the two points and we were ahead 14 to 13 with 42 seconds to go on the clock, and we were beaten by two touchdowns. If anyone had asked me how it happened, I could not have told them. It had been a nightmare from start to finish.

* * *

Three seasons before this game, I had gone to my superintendent during the middle of the season.

"Paul, I plan on retiring from football coaching at the end of this season," I had told him.

"What kind of season will we have next year Floyd?" he asked.

"Terrible," I answered. "Our material the next three years is going to be mighty thin, and victories are going to be hard to come by."

We were competing in a tough league with many larger schools. To make matters worse, we were the only community in our league that had a parochial high school with an athletic program. Therefore we were playing without our Catholic boys, and playing against teams with their Catholic boys.

However, we had been holding our own with these other tough teams through better and more stringent training rules, and very aggressive play. However, the future for the next three years did not look very bright.

"Floyd," Paul theorized, "if we bring in a new coach now and he has three losing seasons, we will have to fire him. Why should you quit now and put that kind of pressure on me and the school board? Your reputation is such that you can survive."

"Listen, Paul," I interrupted, "when I came down here to

start coaching, the material was very lean. I took my licks and built it up. Now I want to retire as a winner. I will still continue to coach basketball."

"That doesn't seem fair, Floyd," Paul replied. "You always said that this school system and community had treated you so well. And now you want to pull out when you have a real opportunity to help us over a rough spot."

I couldn't say "no" to that, and I told him I would take football three more years. I would attempt to hire and train a man to take over after that three years.

We hired a brilliant young man, one of my former athletes at Coldwater. Bill had just graduated from Western Michigan University after a super football career with many honors. Bill was an intelligent man and an excellent math teacher, as well as a great competitor in athletics.

After I finished my three year stint, Bill became head football coach for two years. Everything seemed to go wrong for him including many injuries to his players. Bill, being a former local star athlete, was open to much criticism from people who knew him.

The pressure kept building up to replace Bill with another head coach. As athletic director, I stood firm that Bill was an asset to our school system and community as head football coach in spite of the losing record. The losses were not Bill's fault.

Since the local downtown "Quarterbacks" could not talk to me about it because I refused to listen, they applied all the pressure on the superintendent, my friend, Paul.

During mid season, Paul called me into his office for a conference. "Floyd," he started, "you know there is a lot of pressure in this town to fire Bill as football coach?"

"Hey, I know it," I answered. "But I am not that concerned about pressure. I am analyzing the situation intelligently rather than through emotional upheaval. I know Bill is a good coach and teacher, and he's a real asset to our system in spite of the won-loss record."

"Floyd, why are we not winning then?" Paul asked. "Tell me what is wrong with our football program. I want to know the reasons we are not winning."

"Well, here we go, Paul," I answered. "Listen carefully. First of all have you noticed what an excellent team our local St. Charles high school team is having each year? Bill is fighting the same problem I have for years. There are several players on those St. Charles teams who would make us a championship team. Do you realize that all of our opposing schools have these Catholic players?

"In fact, I looked at Three Rivers' starting lineup, and ten out of their starting eleven were Catholic boys. Do you know that if you removed those ten from the Three Rivers lineup and filled our lineup with St. Charles boys that could help us, we would have drubbed Three Rivers by 50 points instead of losing to them.

"However, Paul, I helped St. Charles start their athletic program years ago. I knew that it would give many more boys of this community an opportunity to have the advantages of playing sports. Are we concerned about the boys of this community or building a won-loss record for the downtown quarterbacks?"

"Besides this," I continued, "Bill has not had adequate coaching help on his varsity."

Paul exploded. "As athletic director why didn't you notify me of this coaching need?"

"Two years ago, Paul, I came to your office and told you specifically that we needed two more strong coaches to help Bill with the varsity. You turned me off, telling me that we already had too many coaches in our school system."

"Floyd, if I knew you really needed these two coaches, I would have approved it in a minute," Paul answered.

"Paul, I didn't come in that day to discuss my health, but to let you know of our coaching needs," I replied. "We lost both Bert and myself off the varsity staff. We didn't replace either one of us, so don't let us put all the blame on Bill." I then walked out of the office.

We lost our next game which was played at our home field. After the game I came down out of the press box, and completed my duties as athletic director including turning off the lights as most of the crowd left.

I was walking across the dark football field when I was intercepted by Paul. "Floyd, I want to talk with you."

"Sure go ahead, Paul, what's on your mind?" I asked.

"What's the chance of us winning any of our last three games?"

"Not very good," I said.

Paul continued, "Is there any one on our staff who could possibly help Bill win one or two of our last three games?"

"Paul, I, myself, could possibly help Bill in the next three weeks of practice. I could possibly straighten out the offensive line, crack the whip on the fellows, and possibly help win one or two of the games," I theorized.

"However, I can not do it, because I am Coach Eby, the former football coach. My attempt to help would amount to taking the team over. This would pull the carpet right out from under Bill. And I won't do it."

"Who is the strongest football coach on our staff, next to Bill?" Paul asked.

"Pat, our freshman coach," I answered.

"Okay, Floyd, I am asking you to assign Pat to the varsity to help Bill the rest of the season, so perhaps we can win a game."

"I won't do it, Paul," I retorted.

"You will do it Floyd, as I am now ordering you to," he said.

"I still won't do it, Paul," I repeated.

"Why not, Floyd?"

"Paul," I continued, "it just does not make sense. Pat is the only coach I have available who is capable of handling fifty freshmen football players. Pat is experienced and knows what he is doing, and if someone is injured, he will do the right things.

"Paul, these ninth grade boys are just as important to their parents as the varsity boys. I will in no way endanger their health to win a varsity football game."

With that final statement, I stalked off the dark football field and headed for the locker room.

We lost our last three games, and the pressure downtown to fire Bill mounted with each loss. Poor Paul was being attacked from every side. They knew better than to come to me. Of course Bill was aware of this pressure and unrest.

I went to Bill. "Bill, you know there is a lot of pressure to replace you as football coach. I want you to know I have and will continue to back you completely. I know you are a good coach, and a real asset to our staff and community."

"I can go all out with my influence and possibly save your job for next year. However, next year doesn't look much better than this year with the returning material. If you want me to, I will do everything possible to renew your contract. All you have to do is say the word. What would you have me do?"

"Coach," he said, "I would rather have you let things fall as they may. Although things have been tough, I am glad to have had the opportunity to work with you these last several years."

Although I notified Paul and the Board of Education that I still believed that Bill was the best man for the job, I did not pressure the Board and Paul to keep him.

I did notify Paul that I would not have anything to do with the selection of the new Coach.

"That's just the way I want it, Floyd," Paul replied. "I want to select this new coach myself."

Paul contacted several universities. After receiving recommendations from the head football coaches at these universities, he decided on an all American football player from Michigan State. Paul let me read the recommendation for Cliff from the head football coach at Michigan State. The recommendation was tremendous. It just seemed too good to me. How anyone could be that good, was hard to believe.

Upon the recommendation of Paul, the Board of Education hired Cliff as our new head football coach. Cliff was an outstanding man in many ways. He was a good looking, well-built young man with an outstanding athletic record. He had many assets. However, he was strictly big time, and should have been a college coach, not a high school coach.

Cliff visited me after he was hired. He told me how he had taken his first job up north for two years, and how he had built a winner from nothing within that two years.

I was not impressed. I always felt that if a person was of outstanding ability, he didn't have to tell it, but it would eventually show. The purpose of Cliff's visit to me was to notify me of the need for new uniforms.

"Mr. Eby, I have been looking over our present uniforms, and I find them very inadequate. I believe that how a team is equipped affects their play. I want to buy all new uniforms for the varsity. I want to buy the best, similar to the uniforms we used at Michigan State."

"Cliff," I said, "we work on a very limited athletic budget here. We have to survive on the amount we take in at the gate. Therefore, we have a budget for each sport and we know how much we can spend each year.

"We have never been subsidized by the taxpayer through the Board. Our football budget for next year will allow for some new uniforms and other equipment, but we will in no way be able to survive that type of purchase."

"Well, Mr. Eby," Cliff replied, "that is what I have to have to turn this football program around and produce a winner, and I must have it."

"Then Cliff, you will have to go beyond me," I told him, "because we do not have that kind of money."

"That is just what I will do, Mr. Eby," he said, as he walked away.

Cliff went to Paul and the Board of Education agreed to subsidize the new uniforms. Cliff purchased some real first class uniforms of the college style, including mammoth college-type shoulder pads. The football squad really looked sharp, and appeared especially large with those shoulder pads.

Cliff believed that his squad members should be conscientious about their school studies. He insisted that he would only have gentlemen represent the Coldwater High

School football team.

Of course, this went right along with our current policy. I was happy about his desire to require his squad members to follow high standards of conduct, including training rules.

Cliff believed that the first important step in producing a winning football team at Coldwater High was to completely sell his squad members on his particular system of football.

"Fellows," Cliff said to his squad, "the football system we are going to use is patterned after Michigan State, and is really unbeatable. These other league teams will not be able to stop it. It is too powerful and deceptive for them. The system itself will win five of our eight games. We, as a squad, only have to win three games to be undefeated because my system will win the other five games."

Cliff was a good salesman, and he had every player believing completely in his system and in his coaching ability.

Big Mike, our fullback, came to me. "Coach Eby, our new football coach is just great. The system we are using is unstoppable. Coach has told me that no one will be able to stop me in this system. We will run up score after score. Isn't this exciting, Coach Eby?"

"It sure is, Mike," I replied. "I am glad you like the new coach and his system."

Cliff stopped me in the hall one morning. "Mr. Eby, I want you to hire two officials for Friday night's pre-season scrimmage with Kalamazoo at our Cardinal Stadium. We are advertising it, and expect a large crowd which will add to our momentum and enthusiasm. It is very important that we win this scrimmage. We want everything organized just like a real game."

"Cliff," I said, "we cannot do this. Our state rules will not allow it. This scrimmage must be on an informal basis with no score kept, no advertising, no paid officials, no kickoff, and no reporting. According to state rules, this is just a practice session."

"Mr. Eby," Cliff broke in, "we are going to play this scrimmage under game conditions. I want you to hire two officials to keep the game under control." Cliff then went to his class.

I immediately called our state director. "Charlie," I said, "our new football coach wants to hold this pre-season scrimmage this Friday night at Coldwater. He wants to have actual game conditions such as hired officials and kickoff, and he wants to keep score."

"Eby, are you crazy?" Charlie asked. "You know our rules and you know this is all illegal. How come you are having it at night? It is supposed to be held at regular practice time."

"Well, Charlie," I answered, "our coach has a practice in the afternoon, and another one each night."

"Okay," Charlie answered, "you can have it at night, but I don't want any hired officials, advertising, kickoffs, or keeping score. I am surprised, Eby, that you would even call me on this, because I know you know the rules."

"I know, Charlie," I countered, "but I wanted you to tell me so I can say it came directly from our state director."

The scrimmage went as scheduled on Friday night, but with the necessary limitations to make it legal. I told Cliff that the state director would suspend our team for the season if we didn't follow the pre-season scrimmage rules.

Coldwater took possession of the ball first on their own twenty yard line. The first offensive call was a handoff to Mike, our fullback, off the right tackle. Big Mike took the hand off fully expecting to run eighty yards for a touchdown with this unstoppable system and unbeatable coach.

As Mike received the handoff, a huge Kalamazoo tackle and a blitzing linebacker simultaneously lowered the boom on him, two yards back of the line of scrimmage. Mike slowly strugged to his feet, shaking his head, not hurt but confused. How could this happen? He didn't believe it. It must be a mistake and a fluke.

He went back to the huddle and the quarterback called his play again to the opposite side. The very same thing happened, and there went Mike's faith in the system and in the new coach.

We were drubbed unmercifully all night by a good

Kalamazoo team during this pre-season scrimmage. Cliff had a thirty-minute meeting with his squad on the field after the scrimmage in an attempt to restore their faith in the system.

The day of our regular season opening game at Hillsdale, we had our usual pep student assembly in our auditorium. Our new coach was in charge of the program, because he wanted to be sure that the student body would get started on the right foot in supporting the team.

Cliff showed his ability as a psychologist and promoter. He staged a real vaudeville act with his football squad on the stage that afternoon.

I sat in the 5th row from the front. I couldn't believe my eyes and ears as I watched what was going on. Cliff built the theme around the idea of forgetting the past defeats, and toward the belief that the future was now.

"We are going to win, win, win!" He made an issue of the new uniforms, and how that was going to inspire the boys to play winning football.

Cliff brought two of his players on stage, both of them dressed in football uniforms. One of our largest players was dressed in one of our brand new uniforms. The other was one of our smallest players dressed in the lousiest football equipment that we had discarded some years ago but was still in our storage room. It looked terrible.

He had both boys, who had gym outfits under their football uniforms, undress one piece of equipment at a time, alternating and comparing each piece of equipment. First the helmet, then the jersey, shoulder pad, hip pad, and then the pants.

"Students and faculty, how would you expect players to win dressed in this kind of equipment?" Cliff asked. "Do you think there is any way we are going to lose to Hillsdale in our tremendous uniforms?"

Sitting out in front, at this stage of the program, I, as athletic director, was feeling sick and humilated.

Cliff then brought the five largest players on his squad out on the stage and lined them up facing the student body as two tackles, guards, and center. The five of them really looked huge and impressive in those new uniforms with the huge college type shoulder pads.

"Now, students and faculty, if Hillsdale starts making some yardage tonight, I will put these five into the game on defense. Do you see how they could make any yardage then?"

I looked at the five on the stage, and I said to myself, "Eby, perhaps Cliff really knows what he is doing. Maybe Hillsdale doesn't have a chance." This Cliff was even getting to me, and convincing me that we were going to win big.

However, I knew these five boys personally. Two had never been out for football before, and the other three were nice kids. But in spite of their size, football just wasn't their game.

But Eby, I thought, perhaps Cliff has changed them. He certainly is a great salesman. I wouldn't miss this game for anything.

After the asembly, Cliff met with his varsity squad in the gym. He had them sitting on the floor as he talked to them to further build up their ego and confidence. As I walked across the gym to go to the locker room I heard him telling them, "Fellows, Coldwater almost beat Hillsdale last year. I just know that we are so much more powerful this year with this new system and a winning attitude. We should really beat Hillsdale tonight 50 to 0. This will be a great night for us, and it will start the season off with a bang."

Cliff had done away with our freshman football squad. We always had a large freshman squad of 40 to 50 players handled by a separate freshman coach with a separate game schedule.

However, Cliff wanted to handle all players by himself and one other coach. He wanted to be sure that all players out for football were indoctrinated with his policies and winning attitude. So Pat, our former freshman coach, drove over to Hillsdale with me to watch the game from the stands.

Cliff, in making sure that the squad was dressed just right, and that everything was perfectly organized, was late leaving the locker room for the playing field. The officials hit the

Coldwater team with a 15 yard penalty on the opening kickoff for arriving late.

On the first play from scrimmage, Hillsdale's halfback ran 62 yards for a touchdown.

Pat, sitting directly behind me in the stands, tapped me on the shoulder and commented, "I don't understand how that Hillsdale player can run so fast in an old uniform."

We lost the game 24 to 6.

Cliff had his squad members clean the Hillsdale locker room until it was spotless. They even mopped it. The Hillsdale athletic director told Cliff that it was unnecessary, but Cliff told him that he wanted to leave it that way.

That weekend Cliff traveled to East Lansing to visit the head football coach at Michigan State who had been Cliff's college coach. Cliff gave his former coach the data and scouting report on Albion who was our next week's opponent. The head coach devised a special defense for Cliff to use against Albion. We played Albion at home on Friday night, and we were defeated 51 to 0.

We then lost to Lakeview 40 to 0, Adrian 48 to 12, and Marshall 39 to 7.

Cliff had a weekly radio program on the local radio station. After five straight defeats, Al from the radio station was interviewing Cliff on the program.

"Coach, in a pre-season interview on this program, you stated that our Coldwater football team was going through this season undefeated. You said that with the material you had, and your new football system that you were sure that no one on the schedule could beat us. Now after the first five games, we have not won a single game. We have been defeated by astronomical scores. What has gone wrong, anyway, Coach?"

"Well, Al," Cliff replied, "I was really sincere when I told you that. After looking at the size and speed of the material I have here at Coldwater, and knowing what my new system can do, I could not see how we could lose a single game. However, I now realize that these varsity players have not been taught any football fundamentals in the past."

Of course, the former football staff and I were listening to the program, and this statement did not help to create harmony on our athletic staff.

We lost our next two games to Three Rivers 13 to 0, and to East Lansing 28 to 12. The last game of the season was against our arch rival Sturgis on our own field. In addition it was to be "Dad's Night."

The fathers of all our varsity players traditionally were invited to one game each year, to sit on a special bench next to the players' bench. Each Dad had the jersey number of his son on the back of his coat, and each was introduced at half-time with his son. This tradition still continues at Coldwater.

Cliff had selected the last game of the season with Sturgis for Dad's night. Big Mike, our fullback, had completely lost faith in our new coach and the new system from the very start of the season. Therefore, he had seen very little playing time, and he wanted to quit the team. I talked him into staying and finishing the season, and persuaded him not to be a quitter.

On the day of the Sturgis game, Coach Cliff came in to my third hour study hall and asked me if he could hand out football jerseys to the varsity football players in my study hall. He wanted the players to wear their jerseys the rest of the day to stir up enthusiasm for the Sturgis game and Dad's night.

"Certainly Coach," I replied, "I think that is a great idea."

Frank called the varsity players up to the front one at a time to receive their jersey. The last one to be called up was Big Mike. All the other players were given their nice new game jerseys. As Big Mike approached the coach, Cliff threw an old decrepit jersey at Mike.

"There is your game jersey, Mike."

The coach had been disgusted with Mike's lack of cooperation.

Mike threw the old jersey right back at Cliff. "Keep your old jersey. I won't wear it and humiliate my Dad."

Cliff hurried over and grabbed Big Mike by the right arm. "Listen, Mike, you are coming to the principal's office with me."

Big Mike pulled his right arm out of the coach's grasp and shouted, "Let go of my pitching arm. I'm not going anywhere with you."

Big Mike was an excellent pitcher on the baseball team. Cliff left for the principals' office by himself and I told Mike to sit down. In a few minutes, I was called into the principal's office by Karl, my boss.

"Floyd, as athletic director I expect you to severely punish Mike for his open rebellion to Coach in your study hall," he commanded.

"I will not do it, Karl," I replied. "Cliff did not use good sense in embarrassing Mike in front of the study hall by giving him a lousy old jersey for the game. If Cliff felt that Mike wasn't cooperating, he should not have allowed him to dress for the game. As long as Cliff had decided to allow him to be dressed for Dad's night, then he should have given him his regular game jersey like he did to the other players."

Karl agreed. Cliff decided to dress Big Mike that night and gave him his regular jersey. He also put Big Mike on the starting lineup in our last game.

Although we lost to Sturgis 12 to 0, Big Mike had a great night. Through his great defensive play, Big Mike kept Sturgis from scoring three more touchdowns. Coach gave Big Mike the game ball which was illegal by state rules. I had to take the ball away from Mike so he wouldn't be ineligible for basketball and baseball.

Paul and the Board of Education had given Coach Cliff a three year verbal contract. This had stuck in my craw. I had asked for a two year contract at one time. They had refused me on the grounds that they never do give more than one year.

One morning Cliff contacted me in the hall at school.

"Mr. Eby, I want to ask your advice on an important matter. I had promised myself and the Board that I would stay here at Coldwater for at least three years, and turn the football program around into a winner.

"However, I have just been offered a job out east in a college. I am now torn between breaking my promise to the Board, and taking this new job, or staying and completing the job I have started here. What do you think I should do?"

"Cliff, you have to take advantage of an opportunity when the door opens," I said.

Cliff took the new job.

* * *

During the relating of these above experiences, I have not intended to degrade in any way my superintendent, principal, Board of Education, or our football coach. All of them are outstanding men with a sincere desire to provide quality education for our children. I love all of them. Our football coach found his calling in new jobs in which he was very successful.

* * *

A few years later, I retired from basketball coaching and as athletic director. I had announced my retirement a year in advance. I had made up my mind that I was going to retire from athletics at the end of my 25th year.

I thought I was going to have a good basketball team and go out a winner. However, Pete and Jack, two of my best returning players, were unable to play. Both of the boys were not only good players but good citizens. Both were going with two fine girls with intentions of culminating their relationship with marriage. The two couples made the mistake of being with each other too often and too long and pregnancy dictated a much earlier marriage than had been anticipated.

I was disappointed, naturally, because this meant that my last year would be mediocre instead of finishing my coaching career with an excellent team. I was not angry with the kids, because I still loved all four of them.

When my wife took a wedding present down to Jack and Mary, Mary told her, "Naturally, Jack felt bad that he couldn't play his last year. However, Jack's greatest regret was that he had let Coach Eby down on his last year."

How can you be angry with kids like that?

During this last year, many teams were having pre-game or half time ceremonies honoring my many years of coaching and retirement.

Before our game at Sturgis, they honored me with a gift and much praise, and then beat us 102 to 67. My good coaching friend Dave at Sturgis didn't pour it on. Instead, he took his regulars out in the middle of the third quarter. But the substitutes hit a greater percentage than the starters. They really had a hot night.

* * *

"Hey Joe, what's the big idea, placing our team on the sideline bleachers instead of at the end of the court?"

I was talking to Joe, the athletic director at Marshall High School during the reserve game between the two schools.

"You know, Joe, you promised me this summer that we could sit our team at the end of the court in this game at your place. You said you would agree to this because it would be my last game ever at Marshall."

"I know, Eby," Joe replied, "but my varsity basketball coach Don, would not consent to it."

I immediately turned to Don. "What kind of a man are you anyway to countermand my request to your athletic director? I really don't know what difference it would make to you."

Don hung his head, and said he would just rather not.

"Okay, you guys, if that's the way you want to act, but I hope you have better hospitality from us when you come to our place. I think your attitude stinks."

I stalked off and went back and sat down on our bench with our reserve Coach Pat.

I never liked to sit on the sidelines with my team, but rather at the end of the court like we did at Coldwater. On the sidelines people were always walking in front of us, blocking our vision on the court. The fans were right back of us and giving us a bad time. When I chewed a player out, they could hear me. When I was discussing strategy with my players and coaches, the fans would mock me.

At the end of the 3rd quarter of the reserve game, I left the bench and started for the locker room to supervise the dressing and preparations for the varsity game. At the end of the court, I ran into Joe and Don again. By this time I had felt bad about how I had talked to them.

I felt compelled to say, "Joe and Don, I am sorry the way I acted about the seating arrangement of our team. This is your home game and you have the right to make arrangements as you see fit. I should be willing to accept your arrangements. And I do."

"You won't like this either, Eby," Joe replied, "but after the initial warmup you will have to take your team to the locker room for a few minutes as we prepare for something special. I know you don't usually do this, but we insist this time."

"Okay Joe," I answered, "you won't hear any more complaining from me about it."

As I readied my team to go out on the court for the initial warmup, I instructed them, "When I tell you, we will come back into the locker room for a few minutes. Joe has some kind of crazy ceremony or promotion going on."

After the warmup and after we went back into the locker room, I gave my team their final instructions and sent them out for the opening tipoff. As I followed my team out of the locker room, I first noticed several chairs at the end of the court plus a large church pulpit chair. I also noticed the cheerleaders wheeling a cart out with a large cake on it.

Signs were being held up, honoring Coach Eby and his retirement.

Boy, did I feel like a bum, and was I embarrassed for the way I had been acting! I did Praise God because I had at least told Joe and Don I was sorry before I went to the locker room. Everyone was nice to me, and I felt terrible about my attitude.

We played a lousy game, but we still won. Afterwards the Marshall School put on a party for the two teams, cheerleaders, coaches, and special friends.

"Dear Lord, why do I have to be so dumb?"

* * *

"Pat," I spoke to my reserve coach, "I am going to sit real still and quiet on the bench tonight. Since this is the last game I ever will coach at Coldwater, I know the crowd is going to be watching me. I am going to fool them by being very refined and dignified."

We were playing Marshall in our last regular season game at Coldwater, and my last home game before my retirement. Our school and fans, cheerleaders, and players had a pre-game ceremony where they presented me with a special plaque, a lifetime pass to all athletic contests, and five gallons of ice cream, my favorite food.

The boys played an excellent game that night, and we defeated Marshall handily. Our team really hustled. They ran everywhere they went, including to the scorer bench, jump balls, foul lines, and to the time-outs. It was a real game of "race horse" basketball and so exciting to me. It worked out just the way I wanted, to end up my coaching career at Coldwater High School.

I told Pat after the game, "I really never got off the bench once tonight during the excitement. I sure fooled people who were expecting me to get excited," I bragged.

"You did much better Coach," Pat said. "You only jumped around several times."

"I didn't get off the bench even once, Pat," I said. "You're as blind as the officials."

Unknown to me, the local paper had a special photographer taking pictures of me all night. The next day the paper had a full page of action pictures showing me jumping off the bench, chewing out the officials, and having many emotional outbursts of joy and sorrow. I then realized how emotional I must have been during my entire career when I was not even trying to control myself.

The Coldwater Jaycees ended my retirement with a special honor banquet for my wife, Betty, and me.

"Coach, we don't want you and your wife to come over here until we come by and pick you up," the Jaycee chairman ordered.

We waited and waited and I told Betty that they had probably forgotten us. When they finally picked us up and escorted us into the Masonic Hall, it was all dark except for the spotlight focused on Betty and me. About 350 people were clapping and then the lights were turned on. People from all over the United States were there, including friends, coaches, relatives, and former players.

During the entire banquet I felt inadequate and undeserving, and sort of embarrassed by all the attention, because I knew I didn't really deserve it. However, I praise God for all my friends, and I love each and every one of them.

I thank the Lord for allowing me to live and work in such a wonderful community as Coldwater, Michigan, and for being able to work with so many wonderful boys and girls in the school system.

God is good to give an undeserving guy like me such a wonderful family, community, country, vocation, athletes, coaches, relatives, friends, and brothers and sisters in Christ.

"Know ye not that they which run in a race run all, but one receiveth the prize? So run, that ye may obtain."
1 Corinthians 9:24

10

A TOUGH BRAND OF DISCIPLINE
...HEADLINE-MAKING SPORTS

Clearly, Coach Floyd Eby set out to win games --- not to make history in basketball and football, although the overwhelming evidence we have is that he did both.

Coach Eby is the only high school coach in Michigan basketball history to win two state championships in two different classes in two different schools.

Such innovations as the full court zone press and race horse basketball, out of which came the one-handed jump shot essentially to expedite his new brand of fast momentum in the game; the open huddle in football "to keep the guys from talking their heads off in a regular huddle"; the split-T as a method of throwing the other team off timing --- certainly these and other innovations were unheard of in his part of the country. Until we see proof to the contrary, we believe they were firsts --- period. The following newspaper stories seem to substantiate our belief.

We are grateful to the newspapers in Michigan who

permitted us to share with you the kind of excitement Coach Eby generated in the sports world during his career.

In addition to surprise-package plays, Eby was a strict disciplinarian. He believed there was no substitute for physical conditioning. Further, he was just as concerned about a player's conduct off campus as he was about his attitudes and conduct on campus. He was intolerant of rule infractions, particularly if breaking a rule had anything to do with a player's basic character development. The following letter to parents of athletes is only one example of Coach Eby's attitude about his athletes: (The Publishers)

Dear Parents;

This is a form letter written to every squad members parents. We are happy to have your son as a member of one of our athletic squads. You may be assured that we will do everything in our power to improve and protect his health at all times. The benefits of participation in athletic sports are too numerous to mention here, but certainly he will gain desirable qualities from sports that he may never have the opportunity to obtain elsewhere. We assure you that we require and demand the highest standards of conduct and the practicing of good habits.

We cordially invite you to attend all our contests, especially the ones in which your boy may participate. We know from past experience that for a boy to have his parents watching him while he is excelling in some physical activity is one of the best boy-parent relationships.

We would like to ask your cooperation and encouragement in the enforcement of the training rules. The following training rules were set up for the school year 1954-55 by the Coldwater High School coaching staff, and have been presented to and approved by the Board of Education. These training rules went into effect March 25, 1954 and will be enforced by the coaching staff. All violators will be punished according to the rule violated and punishment indicated for such violation. The training rules are as follows:

1. *Training rules are in force the year around including the summer. Any boy breaking training rules at any time during the year will be a violator and will be punished. A summer, or between season violator's punishment will apply to the first sport he intends to go out for following the violation. NOTE: A violator does not necessarily have to be seen by a coach. The coaching staff may use evidence from any source they feel is reliable.*

2. *The use of alcohol and tobacco is not tolerated. Any squad member on first offense will be eliminated from the squad for the remainder of the season. He may go out for another sport providing he can convince the coach concerned that he will stay in training. However, it will be each coach's perogative to refuse the violator the right to participate in any sport if he believes that the violator would be destructive to the squads morale and training!*

NOTE: All squad members must be responsible for their own training. The fact that a boy has been eliminated from the squad for the same offense that another squad member is getting by with, will carry no weight in lessening his punishment. The violator has broken the rule and must be punished. No violator will be left on the squad when the coach has proof that he is a violator. However, it may be impossible to obtain proof on all offenders, but all offenders caught will be punished.

3. *Squad members responsible for stealing, vulgar and obscene language, and other immoral practices will be removed from sport participation by the Athletic Director or coaching staff.*

4. *Every squad member who is dressing for the next days contest must be home by 10:00 p.m. the night before a contest unless he has special permission from a member of the coaching staff or some other eligible reason. Special curfews may be set by the coach concerned.*

5. *Boys making squad trips to other towns will be held strictly accountable for their conduct and any individual guilty of such misconduct may be removed from the squad and game participation upon the discretion of the Athletic*

Director or coaching staff.

6. Effective April 1, 1954, any Coldwater athletic award winner including varsity, reserve, and future varsity, who uses tobacco or alcoholic beverages while wearing his athletic award will not be eligible to win any more athletic awards at Coldwater High School. Even if properly reinstated on an athletic squad, he has forfeited his right to win an award in that sport.

Please take time to go over this letter with your son. Also please feel free to telephone, write or see us personally on any problem concerning your boy. We are interested in your son.

E. Byron Thomas　　　　　　　　　　　　　　*Floyd Eby*
[Superintendent]　　　　　　　　　　*[Director of Athletics]*

Lansing State Journal, 1940

STATE Journal

SPORTS

Williamston Basketball-mad As Team Plays for the Title

By ED KITCHEN

Williamston's 1,500 population was basketball-mad today. Mad, because on the Jenison fieldhouse floor in East Lansing tonight at 7:15 o'clock the best cage team ever produced at Williamston high school will tangle with Keego Harbor to decide Class C supremacy of the lower peninsula of Michigan.

For Williamston it is a happy day to be standing on the titular threshold. For its boyish coach, Floyd Eby, who in his first year out of college has guided the Hornets to 21 victories in 22 games and a place in the championship bracket, it is even a happier one.

The rise of Williamston under Eby has been nothing short of meteoric. Fresh out of Michigan State college in 1939, Floyd took over the grid coaching job at Williamston last fall and guided his charges to the Ingham County league title. Then he picked up the cage reins and coupling common sense with good material has brought the Hornets where no one would have admitted possible two months ago.

After deadlocking with Holt for the county championship in regular season action, Williamston went on to turn back Dansville, Holt and Okemos in the Leslie district tourney, then Nashville, Litchfield and Jackson St. Mary's in the Albion regional and finally Wyandotte St. Patrick's and East Jordan in the state meet proper.

There is no black magic in Eby's winning formula. The Hornet mentor, who might be mistaken for one of his own players, points out that his boys win because "they outrun and outjump their opponents, and they make baskets." It's as simple as that.

Passing, Eby believe, plays an important part in the Hornets' attack, but it is not so important as speed. Floyd is surprised to be "up there," but was not amazed when his boys began to roll over tournament

A TOUGH BRAND OF DISCIPLINE/171

foes because he believes they hit the peak at midseason.

Like most good teams, Williamston's attack revolves around one brilliant performer. That lad is Ron Stover, the loping, dead-eye forward who has counted 341 points in 22 games this year. In four years of competition at Williamston he has scored 856 points. This season he has counted 30 points on one occasion and last year collected 35 in one game.

Stover plays a "basket-hanging" role for the Hornets. He plays his man loosely on defense and then zooms down the floor under a long pass if his mates gain possession of the ball. Williamston's zone defense is extremely effective and is made to order for the team's fast-break attack.

Stover, a senior who furnishes plenty of food for argument when compared with Dave Latter, Leslie's smooth worker, isn't the whole Hornet team by any means, however. Four juniors, Dean Gaffner, Oland Dunkel, Dick Hagerman and Dick Wells, are the other starters, while Bob Ridenour, Irvin Offill and Roland Dunkel furnish capable reserve material.

This is the group which will battle it out on the Jenison floor tonight for the Class C headpiece, and if the support of all of Williamston means anything — they'll win it.

Lansing State Journal, 1940

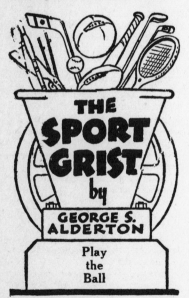

THE SPORT GRIST by

GEORGE S. ALDERTON

Play the Ball

STUDENTS of basketball who watched Williamston successfully storm the Class C basketball heights in the state tournament are still discussing the Hornets. Unorthodox is the word that most of the technical minds applied to the new champions.

Certainly no tournament in years has seen a team that played its basketball quite like the boys from Billtown. Especially on defense did they differ from other contenders.

Many of those who attempted to analyze the team decided that it was their unusual style of defense that made them difficult to defeat. Their system, if they had one, is best illustrated by something that happened in one of the regional games at Albion.

Williamston was having quite a struggle against one of the regional opponents and the tension was high. The timer's horn sounded and out dashed a substitute from the Williamston bench. One of the game officials reached out and seized the boy's arm.

"Do you know who your man is?" he asked solicitously of the excited substitute.

The boy flashed a reply at once.

"We don't have to get a man," said the lad. "We play the ball. Let's go!"

And anybody who watched the Class C kings in action will testify to the truth of his statement. If there was one thing that Williamston did in a large way it was to play the ball. The moment the other team got the leather, five Hornets descended and buzzed angrily about the possessor of the ball until he either handed it to somebody else or gave it up. More often than not, he yielded it. The quick and complete descent of the Williamston team upon the player who had the ball frequently rattled the opposition. On one occasion in the East Jordan game, the confused player actually tossed the ball to Referee Eddie Powers who had to sidestep quickly to avoid being struck.

"Play the ball."

That's an old bit of sports philosophy that sometimes is overlooked in this modern day of highly developed defensive technique. Without knowing it, a team gets to playing the man instead of the ball. Maybe Coach Floyd Eby and his boys have something that could be put to use by a lot of other teams.

Constantine Advertiser Record, 1943

FLOYD EBY WILL GO TO COLDWATER

Floyd Eby, Constantine boy who has been a successful coach at Williamston, Mich. next year will be with the Coldwater school. In the following words, George S. Alderton, sports editor of the Lansing State Journal, pays fine tribute to Coach Eby:

"Williamston has lost a good coach, an enthusiastic citizen and a pessimist with the announcement that next September will find Floyd Eby coaching athletic teams at Coldwater. The County league has had few figures in its coaching ranks who would measure up to Floyd in any of the three categories. He has been an efficient, colorful and downcast member of the league's ranks ever since he joined.

"Floyd's ability was recognized by Coach Charlie Bachman in college. As a member of the Michigan State college football squad, Eby was one of a number of centers in the Spartans' Orange Bowl year. He wasn't the best center, either. As a matter of fact, Floyd was quite a way down the list for he didn't have the beef or speed to stay abreast of the parade which in those days were pretty fast. But he had something a lot of others didn't have. He had fire. He was the greatest morale builder on the squad and for that reason, if none other, was carried on trips. Floyd kept his pals in top spirits.

"At Williamston he used the same prescription that worked so well in college. He had a lot of enthusiasm and he had a coaching knack. His teams won in spectacular fashion and with such regularity everybody knew why. But if you stopped and asked him about his teams, his jaw would drop and he would affect the air of a doomed man. Never to our knowledge has he ever admitted he was going to have a thing on the ball. But he always did. The county league will miss him."

The Albion Recorder, 1943

Along The
SPORTS
FRONT

With The Recorder

Coldwater's Basketball Renaissance

When Coach Floyd Eby moved from Williamston to Coldwater last fall, his reputation as a basketball coach was widely known and the choice was hailed as a good one .... At Williamston, Eby always seemed to have at least one high scoring player .... So far at Coldwater, he has been unable to find a player, who, under his "running" style of play, could score ten points in any contest but he has come up with ten players of equal ability so that he has been able to use alternating quintets. and virtually all ten players have broken into the scoring column every night .... Albion's fair to middling team got its first taste of Coldwater's body checking, race horse team Friday night - and did not like it ... But the shock that such a style of ball could be perpetrated left the Albion boys much in the condition of an inland lake swimmer suddenly jumping into the waters of Lake Superior .... Next time, it will be different - perhaps ....All eyes in Albion will be on next Friday's Coldwater invasion of Sturgis ... The odds still are that Sturgis should win on its mammoth court .... If Coldwater should win. Eby may take his boys straight to a championship if Marshall does not intervene.

COULD THEY DO IT WITH TWO OFFICIALS?

After suffering defeat at Coldwater's hands, every team is going to ask if it could happen with two officials on the floor (as the Twin Valley still sticks to the one official system, in contrast with most other state leagues, big and small.)....

Last Tuesday night, Coldwater won a two-official game from Three Rivers 27-22 after having 30 fouls called upon it and five of its players sent to the showers .... Main reason was that Three Rivers, after having won in December at Coldwater, was so shocked at the spectacle that it "lost its fight somewhere along the way" and only made 11 out of 31 free throws.... As the Three Rivers Commercial reported the fray, it was: 'From late in the first quarter onward, it was slam-bang, slip and slide .... It isn't basketball, but its effective - for Coldwater ... The Cardinals' wild style of play caught up Coach Francis Pellegrom's charges in the heat of the thing and the 'Cats unlearned almost what they'd learned about the game of basketball."

THE BEST FORMULA TO BEAT SUCH A TEAM

Probably the best formula to beat such a team is to let bedlam reign in all scrimmages for a week before hand, use football shoulder pads on the more shy players, practice free throws diligently and hire a second official.... If that does not work, there is nothing to be done but grin and bear it .... For, as we said in our original report of last Friday's game, there is nothing vicious or dirty about Coldwater's play.

F.V.M.

Three Rivers Commercial, 1944

COLDWATER CRASHES THROUGH 29 TO 23

Visiting Club Out Tumbles Locals 29-23

Take Contest As Local Combination Goes to Pieces Face of Strange Play

Coldwater out-wrestled and out-scrambled the Three Rivers Wildcats machine last night.

Coldwater's wild style of play caught up Coach Francis Pellegrom's charges in the heat of the thing and the 'Cats un-learned almost all they'd learned about the game of basketball. The result wasn't a happy one for Three Rivers. The score of the thing was 29 to 23, and the best thing that could be said of the Coldwater club was that it had lots of fight, and the worst that could be said of the local club was that it lost it's fight somewhere along the line.

Coldwater has some reason to be proud of the revenge no doubt. It's the first win over a local club since 1938.

Yet, if it was action the fans wanted, they got it. From late in the first quarter onward it was slam-bang, slip and slide. It isn't basketball but it's effective, for Coldwater. Thirty fouls were chalked up against the visitors to 14 for the local aggregation.

Three Rivers went off on top and for up to the last two minutes of the initial stanza had scored a shutout over Coldwater's plungers. It was 5 to 0 with two minutes to go. Then "Double-Ought" Papke scored a field goal and Musser counted a free toss and

Newberry accounted for a tying field goal so that the heat closed in a 5-all deadlock.

Three Rivers looked something like the basketball club it has been previously this season only in this second quarter. It scored nine points to four, and really controlled this section of the madhouse. Losik was in for Snell to start it off. Snell had looked none too good. Martin suffered a cut on the forehead and was derricked and Newberry and Corless both scored buckets to raise the Coldwater count to 9 to 5.

Then Sam Massie collected a free toss and so did Losik and Keefer wafted in a field goal. Keefer's free toss gave Three Rivers its first lead since it gave the original five point advantage away and the 'Cats led 14 to 9 at the half with added help from Slim Tom Craw

who potted a long bucket.

Corless opened things up for Coldwater in the third with a bucket and added a free toss before Lakey gave his club some help with a long field goal. Newberry and Papke counted field goals to knot the score. Papke shot his club into a two point lead with a bucket. Massie and Keefer accounted for three points on charity shots for remainder of the stanza as Coldwater collected another pair of markers to stand 20 to 19 at close of this chapter.

Bandaged and returned Harold Martin made his club's lone three points in the night-mare fourth as Coldwater piled it on, and perhaps the only regrettable thing about the close of this affair from a local standpoint was the fact that the local contestants lack some seven points of being a winner.

MORE LIKE A WRECK THAN BASKETBALL —

...And it is.

Forward Sam Massie is under the pile. He and Coldwater player simultaneously tried for possession of the ball in the final stanza and as both slipped the rest of Coldwater's commandos piled on top as Losik, Keefer and Lakey : (with backs to the camera) and Martin on far side of the fracas, looked on. Coldwater's football style won for 'em 29 to 23.

Commercial photo

176/CHAMPIONS FOREVER

WHAT THE EDITOR THINKS

A Coach and His Philosophy

One of the toughest jobs in a community is coaching a high school team.

That's because there are local politics, Saturday morning quarterbacks, and dozens of other hazards that stack up quite deeply - especially if the local boys are losing. The demand is to win!

Williamston High School once had a coach who piloted a team into a state championship. And we wouldn't mention it except Floyd Eby, now head basketball coach at Coldwater, has a fine philosophy about high school athletics.

"You bet we want to win," Eby is quoted in a Detroit Free Press article, "but under our rules and at our price."

Coach Eby believes that a player must observe the rules and earn the privilege of playing on the team. Eby's rules are reportedly rugged. He sticks by them and insists that the rules come first and winning second.

A year ago two first stringers broke the code of ethics all Coldwater varsity players must sign before they draw equipment. Eby immediately dropped them from the squad. Eby saw his worst season in 20 years.

Williamston folks can recall that Eby absolutely prohibited swearing. But then that was only one of his rules. Here are some other Eby principles:

"Make all the mistakes you care to, but make them only once;

"Use study time to full advantage. An ineligible player hurts his team's chances;

"If you think you are important, quit the team to help it out;

"Don't brag. It isn't the whistle that pulls the train;

"If the team loses, go home immediately and stay home until the next morning;

"Take your choice: Play at night or play basketball."

There is something admirable about this coach and his strong principles. The young athletes today need to be guided by coaches of depth and solid conviction.

It's refreshing to read about a coach who stresses the welfare of the athlete first and the pleasure of the spectator second.

Playing for Profit

★   ★   ★

But Not with Money Deals---Ideals!

BY HAL SCHRAM
Free Press Staff Writer

COLDWATER— In autumn's darkening afternoon hours the monotonous thud...thud...thud ... of a basketball echoes through the corridors of Coldwater's magnificent new high school.

To coach Floyd Eby and his dedicated squad the stacato tattoo pounds out its own challenge: Win ... win ...win!

"You bet we want to win," Eby will tell you, somewhat defiantly, "but under our rules and at our price."

*   *   *

THE RULES under which one earns the privilege of playing basketball for Coldwater High are rugged.

The price in personal sacrifice is high.

In 20 years as a high school coach Eby has earned the respect of all who have played for him. His ideals, his philosophy of teaching, coaching and living come first- his won-lost record second.

Just a year ago Eby envisioned a winning winter for his 1958-1959 squad.

Three experienced seniors were available each bred and branded in the Eby style of race horse basketball - run, fake, shoot, rebound and run, run, run.

* * *

BUT AN INJURY sidelined one of the three veterans before the first game.

A few nights later the other two ran afoul of the law and both were immediately dropped from the squad.

The two boys had broken the code of ethics all Coldwater varsity players must sign before drawing equipment. They had forfeited their right to play.

There was no chance now for a winning year.

Eby went to work with the juniors and sophomores who were still willing to pay his price. Week after week the Cardinals took their beatings in a 2-15 season, the worst in Eby's 20 years as a coach.

* * *

"I THOUGHT I'd die if I ever had a season like that," Eby says now. "But actually things worked out just the other way."

You couldn't help but marvel at the way these kids worked, fought and hung together even when the opposition would double the score."

"Now we're back together and I've never awaited any season as much as I have this one. Perhaps we still won't win any championships, but if we can avoid serious injuries we're going to be tough."

From a pessimistic fellow like Eby these are words worth worrying about for opposing coaches.

As thorough and demanding as Eby is in his coaching and conditioning, once that whistle blows his squads are magnificently unpredictable.

* * *

Floyd Eby

COLDWATER may pin you under a full-court press for a while, switch to its famed zone-box-with-a-chaser and then choose to be as docile as a kitten long enough to lull you into complacency.

'You have to have faith in the press," Eby insists. "You have to live with it until it becomes an instinctive pattern. You must have an adequate cover-up system or you'll get killed."

Eby's offensive theory is one of

basic simplicity.

Get to the basket with the shot that will score as soon as you can. You're only going to sink a certain percentage of your shots anyway, so the more you shoot the more points you'll score.

* * *

WHEN EBY first rocked the state with his devilish zone-box-with-a-chaser at Williamston High in 1940, it rewarded him with a state Class C championship in his first year out of Michigan State College.

"Organized confusion" - that's what they called it then.

When Eby went to Williamston he found a marvelous shooter in Ron Stover. But Stover was virtually hopeless defensively.

"Ron wasn't worth a plug nickel on defense, but goodness could he shoot," Eby recalls.

"So we devised the four man box zone and let Ron make a nuisance of himself chasing the ball out front."

* * *

THE INSTANT Williamston gained possession of the ball Ron was on his way. One step ahead of the defense was all he needed. One long full-court pass and Williamston had a basket.

If Williamston scored 40 points, Stover would generally wind up with 32 of them.

Those were the days of ball control, set plays and methodical offensive patterns. There were no pressing defenses, no fast breaks nor hell-for-leather race horse offenses.

Eby admits that there were probably a couple of dozen better teams on the peninsula that year, but Williamston took the most shots and scored the most points.

IT WAS THIS Eby-coached team which first popularized the one-handed jump shot, the defensive press and the run-and-shoot game of today.

When a team can't press effectively it can foul its way right out of the gym. Last year's inexperienced Coldwater team did just that one night in losing to Marshall, 87-49. The Cardinals drew 54 fouls that night.

But the squad is a year older now and Eby feels it has learned its lessons well.

"We should be back to our normal 25-30 fouls a game this winter," he says.

In Rick VanDyke, 6-foot-3½; Gordon Archer, 6-foot-2½ and Dick Holben, 6-foot-1, Eby figures he'll have enough height.

Don't be surprised if Coldwater reverses that 2-15 record of a year ago this winter.

What It Takes To Be a Cager At Coldwater

It is not easy to earn the privilege of playing basketball for Coldwater High School.

Here are a few of the tenets under which athletes live, work and play for Coach Floyd Eby:

1—On days of practice or games you are not to see or talk to girls from 3:10 p.m. to 6 p.m.

2—More bone in your back and less in your head.

3—Referees make fewer mistakes than you do.

4—Make all the mistakes you care to, but make them only once.

5—Use study time to full advantage. An ineligible player hurts his team's chances.

6—Condition counts—and wins! Get tough with yourself.

7—If you think you are important, quit the team to help it out.

8—Don't brag. It isn't the whistle that pulls the train.

9—If the team loses the game, go home immediately and stay home until the next morning. This means you don't go dancing, see your girl or get taken home by a girl.

10—Take your choice: Play at night or play basketball.

Battle Creek Enquirer and News, 1961

Full Press Began by Accident

By BILL FRANK

COLDWATER — More and more high school basketball teams each year change to the all-court press type of defense.

No coach in the state is more responsible for this move than Floyd Eby, the veteran head cage mentor here at Coldwater High School. He has won two state championships with the all - court press (Williamston in 1940, class C) and Coldwater (class B 1949).

Most coaches around the state credit Eby with "inventing" the all - court press. But, Eby will not take full credit for it. He said "Before I

Floyd Eby

decided to utilize the all-court press I noticed that many coaches pressed all over the court late in the game when they were behind!"

There were very few coaches around the country, if any, who utilized the all-court press from start to finish in a game. Eby is believed to be the first. How did he happen to come up with the idea? Eby admits it was by accident, on purpose.

* * *

HE STARTED it back in 1940 when he was finishing his

collegiate work at Michigan State University in East Lansing. His first coaching job was at Williamston High (near MSU).

Eby recalled his first practice session at Williamston. He said: "I called the kids together, gave them the ball and told them to go ahead and scrimmage. I went into the bleachers to observe. I noticed that Ron Stover (star scorer on the team) never went back on defense. He was what I call a basket-hanger."

When he saw Stover do nothing on defense, Eby stopped play and quickly asked Stover: "Who guarded your man last year?"

Eby dismissed practice that day, went to his room and put on his all-night thinking cap.

He wanted to play man-to-man defense but couldn't if Stover couldn't play defense.

As a result of this situation, Eby decided to use a four-man box defense and give Stover the job of acting as "chaser." His job was to chase the man with the ball.

   ✣   ✣   ✣

THIS DEFENSE worked so well the first game that Eby kept improving on it, using it from one end of the court to the other. It turned out that Stover became a key man in the defense. In addition, he set school scoring records in leading Williamston to the state championship.

"Folks were amazed in East Lansing when they saw our type of all-court action from start to finish," Eby recalls.

Despite his early success with the all-court press, very few coaches in the state were sold on the idea. Little by little, after World War II, coaches began to install it.

After his Coldwater team beat River Rouge in the 1949 Class B state championship game, 49-42, Lofton Greene (Rouge coach) told Floyd: "That settles it. If you can win a state title with the all-court press, I'm convinced." Greene has utilized the same defense ever since. He won two state titles with it and is favored to do it again in 1961.

Incidentally, Eby's first team in 1940 also is credited with being the first (at least in midwest) to come up with the one-handed jump shot. This, too, was an accident. He said: "Our kids got to running so fast up and down the court that they couldn't stop to set shoot . . . so, they started tossing the ball one handed."

   ✣   ✣   ✣

Ingham County News, 1962

Bob Tales . . .

By Bob Curry

It was in the fall of 1939 that Floyd Eby appeared upon the ICL sports scene to guide the destinies of the Williamston athletic teams and guide them he did. The ex-MSU athlete led the Hornets to many honors but his most prized possession I am sure is the state Class C basketball championship in 1940.

I honestly believe that Eby did more to revolutionize basketball in Michigan than any man. The conventional type of basketball, the controlled ball offense, if you please, that used to be a thing of beauty and pleasing to watch - well, Eby just threw it out the window. In its place, he came up with the present-day fast break, the so called "race horse" type of assault. The self-appointed "experts" said it wouldn't work - but it did and it brought Williamston of the ICL its first and only state title.

Coach Eby had the "horses" and he knew it - and he made the most of their ability.

Playing on this quintet were the following — Dick Wells, Ron Stover, Oland Dunckel, Dick Hagerman, Dean Gaffner, Bob LaFerrier, Bob Ridenour, Irwin Offhill, Bob Eaton, Roland Dunckel and Harold Price. The team manager was Frank Eaton.

They blasted their way to 13 victories in a 14-game schedule by ringing up 491 points to the opponents' 289 to capture a portion of the ICL title. Webberville fell before the Hornet onslaught 31-18, Haslett 32-16, Stockbridge 24-17 and 46-19, Dansville 40-16 and 39-34, Leslie 44-21, Okemos 39-18, Napoleon 44-30, Perry 37-24 and Brighton 42-17 The lone Williamston loss was sustained at the hands of Holt 28-26 in the second game of the season.

As opponent after opponent felt the ravages of the Hornets' attack and fell by the wayside the "experts" still vowed that the Eby team showing was but a flash in the pan and that soon the world of basketball would return to normalcy. But the hustling Hornets rampaged to a district championship by dumping Dansville 32-22, Holt 33-32 and Okemos 38-30.

Then they swept to the regional title with victories over Nashville, Litchfield and Jackson St. Mary by the scores of 35-21, 33-32 and 32-27 respectively.

Their type of attack was still working despite the scornful jibes of the experts - Wyandotte St. Patrick felt the Hornet sting to the tune of 36-26; East Jordan was a 30-26 victim and then came the "Great Night" in the mammoth Jenison field house as the Ebymen went out to do battle with Keego Harbor for the state's highest honors in the realm of schoolboy basketball.

There were those skeptics who still held steadfast to their contention that it was all a bad dream - that no team could play that type of basketball and win a state title. "Wait till they get to Jenison field house," they choroused, "they won't be able to throw those long passes on that lengthy court - it will be suicide."

If my memory serves me right Keego Harbor never knew what hit them as Williamston proceeded to rack up a huge first-half lead by virtue of their race horse tactics. I can still see Dunckel rifling that ball down court, I can see Stover and Wells pouncing high in the air to gather it in and slip in under to score again and again.

To be sure Keego Harbor's strategy board worked out some changes in their defensive tactics that almost proved the skeptics right as the Keego Harbor cagers gradually closed the gap. I remember it took a last second basket, it might have been Stover, it might have been Wells, it might have been Gaffner or Hagerman or Dunckel, but who cares? Anyway it was a last ditch basket that gave the Hornets of Coach Floyd Eby a 37-35 victory over Keego Harbor, gained them a state championship and proceeded to make the faces of some of the so-called "experts" just a little bit red.

Battle Creek Enquirer and News, 1962

REGIONAL *Sports* ROUNDUP
TWIN VALLEY   CEREAL CENTER
WEST CENTRAL   LITTLE C
BARKENALL   ST JOSEPH VALLEY
CENTRAL MICHIGAN D   KVA

Eby Heads into 24th Season

By BILL FRANK

COLDWATER—Floyd Eby, the resourceful Coldwater High School coach who makes basketball interesting in any number of ways, embarks on his 24th season as a mentor tonight in Marshall where his Cardinals take on Hastings in the unique twin bill opener.

When anything unusual goes on in basketball, it's almost a

certainty that Eby had something to do with it. It was his approval that helped athletic director Joe Cooper of Marshall "cook up" the unusual twin bill varsity opener tonight.

Coldwater and Marshall are the home teams. Coach Eby's Cardinals take on Hastings in the opener while Marshall and Springfield clash in the nightcap.

Floyd Eby

Eby began his career back at Williamston High in 1939 when he was completing his college education at Michigan State. In 1940, Eby guided Williamston to the Class C state title in spectacular style. He employed pressing tactics, a defense new to Michigan cage circles. Now, however, the pressing game is common.

Another State Title

From Williamston, Eby went to Coldwater where he led the Cardinals to the state Class B championship in 1949. Now, for the first time, Coldwater is a Class A school.

But, Eby has no illusions about a Class A title this year. In his usual "optimistic" manner he simply said, "I don't see how we are going to win a game this year." Regardless of what he says, Eby-coached teams never go into a game feeling they are underdogs.

Eby-style basketball is being played throughout the state by teams coached by former Eby players. The list is imposing. Here are the coaches who learned their basketball under Eby and the schools where they coach:

Bill Zabonick and Bob Whitcomb, Bronson; Fred Hobart, Coldwater St. Charles; Wally Dunckel, Haslett; Ken Eckman, Lansing Everett; Rex Corless, Rockford; Joe Grigg, Muskegon Mona Shores, and Doug Mitmesser, assistant at Coldwater High.

Coldwater Daily Reporter, 1963

Veteran Card Cage Mentor
To Retire After Next Season

By SETON BOVEE

Coldwater High School's veteran basketball mentor, Floyd Eby, today announced he plans to retire from active coaching at the end of the 1963-64 season.

"One more year will round out an even quarter of a century," Eby explained, "so I plan to make next year my last as a coach."

After his final season, the Cardinal mentor expects to remain a faculty member and devote more time to his duties as school athletic director.

Coming on the eve of the 1963 district cage tournament, Eby's announcement was no surprise to his closest associates. He has been considering the move for some time but was reluctant to turn over the reins to a new coach until there was more in the way of good cage talent to offer his successor.

Expected Rough Year

He knew in advance that this year would be a rough one at Coldwater. However, with all five starters returning next year along with a fine crop of reserve players, it is expected that basketball will be on the upgrade at Coldwater High during at least the next three years.

In contemplating retirement in another year, Eby can look back with justifiable pride and satisfaction on a coaching job well done. Of course, there is more to coaching than a won-lost record but unfortunately, as far as the public is concerned, that seems to be the most important.

In four years at Williamston and 20 at Coldwater, Floyd's basketball teams have amassed on enviable mark of 224 victories against 164 defeats. His teams have won eight league championships, five district tournament titles, three regional tourney championships and one area crown (in the war year in which gas rationing wiped out the state finals.)

Holds Unique Record

He holds the unique distinction of being the only Michigan prep coach ever to win state champions in different classes at different schools. At least two others have won state titles in two different classes but at the same schools.

His 1940 team at Williamston gave Eby the state Class C championship in his initial year as a coach. His 1949 Coldwater team won the state Class B crown. His longest winning streak was 30 straight while at Williamston.

In tournament competition, Eby-coached teams have won 35 games while losing 18. His present club will be his 21st tournament team inasmuch as he missed two years while on leave of absence to the Navy during World War II.

Eby was the architect of Coldwater's golden basketball era in the late 1940's. His teams then set a new Twin-Valley conference record by sweeping to four consecutive undisputed league crowns. Only Gus Ganakas and his East Lansing Trojans have been able to equal that achievement.

During that period (and even today) Eby's unique full court press and race horse style basketball was the talk of Michigan prep cage circle. It has been copied but never exactly duplicated by other coaches down through the years.

Eby's early successes at Coldwater have worked to his disadvantage in more recent years. Feared by rival coaches, opposing clubs have worked longer and harder for their games with Coldwater.

As Coach Ganakas told us a couple of years ago, "We work harder for our Coldwater games because we never know what Floyd will come up with. And you can depend upon it, he always comes up with something you don't expect."

Who Was Best Athlete?

We asked Eby the other day to name the best athlete he has coached.

"That's hard to say," he replied. "There have been quite a few good boys. There was Ron Stover (star forward on his Williamston team). He was exceptional.

"Pound for pound, and inch for inch I'd have to say Eugene Sowles, (diminutive guard on Coldwater's 1949 state championship five) was one of the finest athletes I've coached.

"But I guess I'd have to say the best was Rex Corless, for his great talent and overall ability."

Eby, incidentally, is proud of the athletes he has coached and who

GOLDEN MEMORIES — This photo of Rex Corless (66) leading Coldwater to victory over River Rouge in the 1949 state Class B final at East Lansing is one of the many pleasant memories Coach Floyd Eby can recall as he contemplates his retirement from coaching one year hence after a quarter of a century in the game. Big Leroy Cox (55) is the other Cardinal in the picture, which was taken by the late Louis B. Keller.

have since entered coaching ranks themselves. The list includes Ken Eckman, Lansing Everett; Oland Dunckel, Haslett; Fred Hobart, Coldwater St. Charles; Joe Grigg, Muskegon Monashore; Rex Corless, Rockford; Bill Zabonick and Bob Whitcomb, Bronson; and Doug Mitmesser, Coldwater.

While better known down through the years as a basketball coach, Floyd didn't do too badly as a football coach either. In four years at Williamston and eight here, his grid teams won 51 games while losing 42. His best year at Coldwater saw him post a 6-2 mark and cop a co-championship. He had three losing seasons, finishing .500 or better the other years.

His Proudest Record

Perhaps the one record, however, of which Floyd is proudest is the fact that Coldwater high school has won the Lloyd F. Kusch memorial good sportsmanship trophy more times than any other Twin Valley conference school.

Eby has stressed sportsmanlike conduct among his players, a fact that hasn't gone unnoticed around the conference.

For instance, after Coldwater had dropped a one-point, last second decision at Hillsdale this season, he received the following letter from William A. Poppink, superintendent of Hillsdale schools:

"Dear Floyd:

"I thought I would drop you a note and tell you that we have always noticed something about the Coldwater teams that pleases me and several other people. This is the fact that whenever a foul is called on one of your boys, the hand goes up and no questions are asked. This has been true for years and I have remarked about it and so have some of our spectators. I feel this is an important element to develop in any team and while you lost the ball game the other night, your boys certainly took it in good style."

Although he plans to give up coaching about one year hence, Floyd will continue to be "coach" to hundreds of boys — many now men — and many others as long as he lives.

Battle Creek Enquirer and News, 1963

—Photo by Norm Burlingame.

MR. PREP BASKETBALL—Coach Floyd Eby of Coldwater High currently is coaching the last team of a colorful 25 year basketball coaching career. He plans to retire after this season.

188/CHAMPIONS FOREVER

Coach Eby Recalls 25 Years of Change

By BILL FRANK

COLDWATER — To watch him guide his team in practice or in a game you never would think that Floyd Eby is coaching in his 25th season.

Coach Eby is just as enthusiastic, energetic and resourceful as he was 25 years ago when he started his prep coaching career at Williamston High School.

Explains Retirement

He is going to retire from coaching after this school year at Coldwater High. Actually, he looks like he could go full steam for another 25 years.

Then, why is he quitting? Coach Eby explained it this way: "I just think that 25 years is a good place to cut off a coaching career. Sure, I hate to quit and give up coaching but I just figure 25 years is enough. I know I'm going to miss it, that's for sure."

Two State Champions

Basketball and Eby go together. Anyone who has played, coached or watched basketball in the Battle Creek area since 1943 has run into the Eby basketball influence. He took over at Coldwater High after four big seasons at Williamston.

Eby is best remembered for winning the state Class C title at Williamston and Class B state crown at Coldwater. He is the only coach in Michigan to win state championships in two different classifications at different schools.

Eby is generally credited with starting the all-court press in Michigan, while at Williamston. He is modest about this claim but adds "I believe we were the first to employ the zone press." Both his state title teams won with the all-court press.

Game Changed Often

Eby's early teams at Williamston also were the first, it is believed, to utilize the one-handed push shot in the state. He said, "I recall in practice that our kids were running up and down the floor so fast that they could not stop to take the recommended two-handed shot ... so, they just let fly with one hand. We worked on it, tried it in a game and it caught on."

Over 25 years the game has changed a great deal. Eby recalls these major changes: From slow, deliberate ball handling to race horse action; change from two-handed to one-handed jump shots; putting in the 10-second restraining line to prevent stalling; change in free throw shooting

A TOUGH BRAND OF DISCIPLINE/189

to bonus rule; **widening the free throw lanes; three seconds rule in the free throw lanes,** and now the **stop-the-clock rule on all violations.**

What does Eby think of all those changes? He said, "I like them. I think they haved helped basketball. The changes have speeded up the game, kept it moving, increased scoring and made it more interesting. However, I think every change has made it tougher and tougher on officials. They have a rough job."

Likes New Rule

About the new "stop-the-clock" rule this season on all violations. Eby said, "I like this rule. It extends the game and gives you more basketball. It helps us one way and hurts us another. It hurts us because we can't fast-break as well and it helps us because we have more time to get our full-court press ready when the ball changes hands in a hurry."

He started this, his final season, with an overall record of 224 victories against 164 defeats in all games. He made these final observations about his coaching career:

"I guess I've been just plain lucky. I've had all the kinds of teams, great, good and not-so-good but I'll say this: I never had a team that never hustled for me and I've enjoyed every second of coaching. I never went into a game with the idea I was going to lose.

"What I'll miss most is the contact with boys. You know, I'm just a country boy at heart. I've turned down offers to coach at big schools and in colleges but I like the smaller town atmosphere where you always feel you are a part of the community.

"One last thing. You know, I was a better football player than basketball at Constantine High and I liked coaching football later but I had more success with basketball. So I stuck with basketball. Believe me, I'm not sorry."

There are a lot of coaches, players and fans who are sorry to learn that Eby is stepping aside.

"Deep down inside I've been concerned with only one major factor in my coaching career - player potential. If my team plays up to its potential then I feel that I have done my job. That's all you can ask of any team."

Coldwater Daily Reporter, 1964

TIME OUT!
━━━━━━━━ With SETON BOVEE ━━━

WE'VE BEEN covering high school sports for the past 35 years and during the last two decades it has been our good fortune to have been closely associated with the man the Coldwater Jaycees plan to honor at a banquet this Saturday night.

Throughout Michigan, Floyd Eby's name has become synonymous with a unique, exciting brand of basketball he originated 25 years ago, and with which he won two state championships at two different schools.

Floyd's career at Coldwater, however, has encompassed more than just teaching his boys to employ a bothersome full court press, and this is the real reason the Jaycees wanted to give him a night of public recognition at the close of his coaching career.

* * *

WHAT WE ARE trying to say was said many years ago by the Duke of Wellington when he declared that "the battle of Waterloo was won on the playing fields at Eton."

Napoleon's conqueror was pointing out a truth that still applies today...that the qualities of leadership, character, and teamwork - so important in meeting all of life's battles - can be taught in the field of competitive sports.

For the past 20 years, Floyd Eby has been teaching these lessons at Coldwater. The fact that his Coldwater teams have earned the respect of their opponents and the men who have officiated their games attests to a job exceedingly well done.

* * *

DOWN THROUGH the years we have known many coaches **more** concerned with their won-lost records than with the future of the athletes they have coached. This is understandable because as everyone knows, there's no one as expendable as a losing coach.

We've admired Floyd for the very things that have drawn criticism from others. He has operated on the theory that his athletes are leaders in the school and should always conduct themselves as such, setting a good example for their fellow students.

He has been unrelenting in training discipline - a fact which has occasionally drawn fire from parents, students and others more interested in winning. His only consolation has been his confidence that a boy once taught he must face the results of his weaknesses, is better prepared for the game of life.

* * *

DURING HIS years as athletic director and coach at Coldwater high school, Floyd has influenced the leisure time activities of some 4,500 boys enrolled in the school's various athletic programs.

On the field, basketball floor and in his personal living, he has set these boys a strong example most of the adults of the community, including us, have been too weak to follow.

In the years we have known Floyd, we have found him to have but one weakness - his love of ice cream. We hope the Jaycees remembered this when they planned the dessert for Saturday night's banquet.

Battle Creek Enquirer and News, 1970

Meet Floyd Eby

Coldwater man leads busy life

By VIRGINIA GUST

COLDWATER — "I guess I'm lucky."

That's what Floyd Eby says in summarizing quite a remarkable career that has been a long series of outstanding successes in a variety of businesses - any one of which would keep an ordinary man straining to do the job.

He's combined years of coaching and teaching with selling real estate, helping to found a new insurance company, building houses, developing subdivisions and launching an area cablevision operation of which he is vice president.

He deplores the idea of taking any credit for his keen business acumen; instead, he attributes his distinctive career to everyone but himself - and to luck.

Eby is a big man. He's amiable, jovial and always has a bit of humor at the ready, and folks find him pleasant company. But, above all, he takes a genuine interest in people.

Always a deeply religious man, Eby says he is gradually shelving his business commitments to devote more time in "doing the Lord's work," as he puts it.

As president of the Gideon Society in Michigan, he spends at least 60 hours a week traveling and talking with the 1,100 Gideons throughout the state.

He pilots his own plane. a Cessna Skyhawk, chalking up about 30,000 air miles annually in his work.

After 30 years of coaching and teaching, Eby retired from the educational field more than a year ago.

"I hated to give up teaching, but I couldn't teach and do the traveling in my work that I needed to do," he said.

He's also getting out of business as soon as he can. "I'm giving it up so I can devote more time to Gideon work," he explained. "The need here is great."

He makes flights both day time and night in his work covering the state. "It's a very rewarding job," he said. "I get weary at times, but I enjoy it. It's something I always wanted to do, and I feel good doing it. This is my future as far as I can foresee," he added.

His coaching and teaching cover a span of 30 years. He coached basketball, football, track and baseball for 25 years. He coached at Williamston for four years before coming to Coldwater High School, where for 21 years he was coach and athletic director. He taught health science the last 10 years before his retirement.

Those closely associated with basketball credit him with starting the all-court press. It was 32 years ago, while he was coaching at Williamston, that he stepped up the relatively slow game and made it into a race horse game by introducing the all-court press which is used now by some high schools, colleges and professional teams.

But, Eby shies away from any credit for the idea and says "the players were responsible for its success."

As basketball coach at Coldwater High School, Eby guided the Cardinal team to its only state championship - in 1949.

Climaxing his long teaching years, he was accorded the honor by the Michigan Education Association as being named "Teacher of the Year" in the state in 1965.

It was while he was in the school system that he began building houses and developing subdivisions.

He has built about 100 houses on a contracting basis, and developed no less than five subdivisions. In fact, he and his wife live at 15 Cardinal Drive, in his first housing development, which was named after the athletic teams of CHS.

His largest housing development is at North Lake. Now, 65 houses are located on what was once 55 acres of farm land. Eby has always handled the layout and platting for his subdivisions.

At North Lake he has taken advantage of the natural contours of the land and transformed them into pleasing building sites on which to construct the exceptionally attractive homes. The development even includes "fish ponds" of spring-fed, clear water.

Eby was never at a loss for names for the streets in his subdivisions. He has used the first names of his two daughters and his three grandchildren.

In one of his housing developments off State Street is a church topped by a white steeple. It's the Good News Bible Center which was opened for worship last year at Easter. Contrary to some thinking, Eby says the church isn't his, and he didn't start it. Rather, he and several families started the church.

"I feel badly about it being called my church, because it isn't" he said, "it's the Lord's church."

About four years ago, he got into the cablevision business. He is vice president of Coldwater Cablevision and his neighbor, Harold Munn is president. There are more than 2,000 subscribers to the service that offers 11 stations plus a weather station. Plans are already under way to expand the CATV coverage with construction of a taller tower near Quincy.

Several years ago, Eby was one of the business leaders contacted to start a new insurance Company in Michigan.

It has since been named the Hamilton International Corp. and in four years has grown from 1,700th place to one of the top 100 in the country. Eby is still a member of the original board and a stockholder.

Born in Camas, Wash., he was raised and went to school in Constantine, southeast of Three Rivers.

His coach and, as Eby puts it, his "idol" was Bruce Gray. Gray later became coach at Marshall High School and, a number of years before his retirement, was superintendent of the Marshall school district. For many years, the two were rival coaches, and Eby looked forward to the competition between his team and Gray's. Eby recalls his French and Latin teacher in school was Mrs. Gray.

Eby was graduated from Michigan State University and during World War II served in the U.S. Navy as a communcations officer.

He likes young people, and they

like him. "Kids are good," he commented, "and are as well behaved as you demand."

He says his present work is a "lot like coaching ... I meet such wonderful, dedicated people in my Gideon work," he said. "I travel around talking to folks and giving them pep talks."

He does admit his life has been a richly rewarding one, but he won't take any credit. "Any success I've had I owe to my folks, the community, the country and my Lord.

"If I could live my life over I would do the same thing. Everyone has been so good to me, good to me in business and I can't say too much for them.

"I guess I'm lucky."

Battle Creek Enquirer and News, 1974

Frankly Speaking
by Bill Frank

Floyd Eby leaves imprint on state basketball scene

IT'S ALL OVER and once again our city and area basketball teams failed to win a state prep championship in any class.

Nevertheless, it was a time to recall better days. Especially for Coldwater fans.

As usual, Floyd Eby of Coldwater took in the state tournament finals on the MSU campus.

He was a central figure.

Wherever he went, fans remarked: "It's been a long time, hasn't it Floyd?"

But to Floyd Eby it still seems like yesterday when he coached his Coldwater High School team to the state Class B championship in 1949.

That was 25 years ago. No team in the Battle Creek area has won a state title since..

Eby held a reunion for his title team recently in Coldwater. Players of the 1949 team who attended included Gene Sowles, Bob Simmons, Gene Fry, Larry Porter, Harry Cooper, Rex Corless, Marv Rosenberg and manager Carlos Clark. Players who could not attend included Fred Weeks, Max McConnell, Jim Rhodes, Bernie Hogoboom, Tom Engle and Leroy Cox.

Eby hasn't coached for a number of years but he always will be remembered as the man most responsible for the all-court press on defense.

He developed the all-court press when he started his coaching career at Williamston High School in 1939-40. In his first year, he guided Williamston to the Class C state championship. He sent shock waves through the crowd with his brand of basketball in the 1940 tournament.

Later, he put Coldwater on the basketball map by guiding the Cardinals to the 1949 state Class B title. He did it by employing the all-court press, a trademark of his teams.

In the 1949 state title game, his Coldwater team beat River Rouge, 49-42. That was a most significant game because it was the first time that River Rouge had reached the title round.

River Rouge coach Lofton Greene, however, went on to become the winningest state title coach in history. His River Rouge Panthers have won 12 state Class B titles, a record for all classes.

Greene credits Eby for his success at Rouge.

Following the 1949 title game, Greene went over to Eby and said,"You convinced me. From now on my teams are going to utilize the all-court press."

Detroit Free Press, 1974

1940 HORNETS 'LIKE PLAYING DEVIL HIMSELF'

Tourney's Original 'Racehorse' Team

By HAL SCHRAM

Detroit Free Press Sports Writer

In the 49 years of the Michigan High School Athletic Association's state basketball championships, the tournaments have survived many obstacles.

For many years, the site was moved around like a game of Chinese checkers from Ann Arbor, to Flint, to Lansing, to Grand Rapids, and back again.

A TOUGH BRAND OF DISCIPLINE/195

When they used the IMA Auditorium in Flint or the Boys Vocational School fieldhouse in Lansing, top crowds never exceeded 6,000 fans.

Then the erection of Jenison Fieldhouse in 1939 turned the glamor on an old show into a sparkling extravaganza.

IN 1940 THE tournament found a permanent home when Flint Northern in Class A, Traverse City in Class B, Williamston in Class C and Weidman in Class D became the first state champions to win in Jenison Fieldhouse.

In 1942, the Red Cedar went on a rampage and flooded the east end of the Michigan State campus. At tournament time, boards were laid down to permit fans to walk over the water and into Jenison for the games.

World War II wiped out the 1943 tournament, but the late Charles E. Forsythe and the MHSAA were back in business in a blizzard in 1945.

Now the finals are threatened by a gasoline shortage, which could keep the fans away. But the tournament will go on as scheduled next week. It has survived everything.

Even Williamston in 1940.

Certainly there have been more thrilling games in tournament basketball than Williamston's 37-35 victory over Keego Harbor in that first Class C final ever to be played in Jenison.

BUT THERE never was a team that did more to revolutionize the game than Floyd Eby's hustling Hornets of 34 years ago.

Race Horse basketball ... the full-court zone press ... the one-handed jump shot .... and the box zone with a chaser (or the 1-2-2 zone) were all born with this team.

Eby was a senior at Michigan State that year and was assigned to Williamston, 10 miles east of the campus, to do his practice teaching. Williamston school officials made him the coach of their basketball team.

There wasn't a six-footer on the club. But Williamston had Eby and a good-natured, love-to-shoot player named Ron Stover.

EBY RECALLS that first practice:

"Not knowing the abilities of my personnel, I divided the players into two teams that first night," Eby recalls. "I gave the manager a whistle and told them to go at it.

"As I watched from the balcony, I noticed Stover staying down at the

Floyd Eby

offensive bucket waiting for his team-mates to throw him the ball. He did not go back on defense.

"I blew my whistle and shouted at him: 'Who guarded your man last year, Stover?' He quickly replied 'McCarrick.' and I asked: 'Who guarded McCarrick's man?" and Stover replied: 'McCarrick."

Eby blew his whistle and dismissed the entire squad. He went back to the dorm to meditate on his problem.

Eby decided that Stover, being a senior, would be most difficult to teach man-to-man defense. But, Eby asked himself, how could his team play with a four-man defense?

EBY DECIDED to use a four-man box zone and make Stover come back and chase the ball out front. The idea brought instant results.

Stover proved a clever, energetic chaser and every time he stole the ball it meant two points, as no one could catch him.

"Ron scored over 400 points in this one season which in the present-day rate of scoring would be close to 1,000 points," Eby said.

Eby found there were many leaks to his one-man press, so he soon sent Stover's half brother, Dick Wells, down to help out, and the two were joined later by Oland Dunckel, Dean Gaffner and Dick Hagerman.

Now Eby had all five zone pressing in the front court, a blessed confusion which was to Williamston's advantage.

The turnovers by the opponents, because of the Williamston chasing game, turned the game into race horse basketball.... chasing, running, shooting and quick rebounding.

"IT WAS LIKE trying to play the devil himself," recalls Frank Crowell, now athletic director at Madison High who was on the East Jordan High team which lost to Williamston in the semifinals.

"We had never seen anything like it," said Crowell. "They jumped away to a 15-20 point lead, which in those days was astronomical, and although we made

The 1940 Williamston High School basketball team, state Class C champions. Back row, left to right: Coach Floyd Eby; Harold Price; Roland Dunckel; Mike Eaton; Irwin Offil; Bob LaFerier; manager Frank Eaton, Front row, left to right: Dean Gaffner; Bob Ridenour; Dick Wells; Oland Dunckel; Ron Stover, and Dick Hagerman.

A TOUGH BRAND OF DISCIPLINE/197

some adjustments at halftime we could never catch them."

Loften Greene, the veteran coach at River Rouge, recalls how he lost to Coldwater [another Eby-coached team] in 1949 when Eby introduced his version of the man-to-man press.

Green said he didn't install run-and-shoot basketball at Rouge until 1950.

Now Eby, in semi-retirement, lives in Coldwater and does much work and traveling on behalf of the Gideon movement.

Coldwater Daily Reporter, 1975

TIME OUT!
With SETON BOVEE

A NEW BOOK was placed on our desk this week and our attention was immediately drawn to its cover which has an excellent color photograph of our long-time friend, Coach Floyd Eby, sitting in the cockpit of his airplane and adjusting his radio earphones.

The title of the book, "Calling God's Tower . . . Come In, Please!" caught our eye next and we could hardly wait to finish our own day's writing to wade into that of Coldwater's newest author.

We've found the book fascinating. It reads just like the man who coached 26 years at Coldwater high school talks . . .straight from the shoulder, no intellectualizing . . . just plain, straight talk.

From the title, you expect it to be about flying and somehow involved with religion. It is partly about flying because Floyd flies some 30,000 miles a year in his own plane, at his own expense, trying to help others find the Christian way of life.

———

EBY DOES NOT claim to be an author and laughingly admits that for a man who holds a Master's Degree from Michigan State, he sometimes murders the King's English. We learned years ago that while Floyd may not be a grammarian, he has the God-given gift of communicating like no one we've ever met.

Yes, his first book is definitely about religion. But to us, it's different, because it is written by Floyd Eby and it takes a profound subject and makes it a deeply personal experience, easy to understand and just as you would expect Floyd to do it.

———————

THERE IS A story behind Floyd's decision several years ago to leave a successful coaching and teaching career, as well as numerous profitable business ventures, to devote his boundless energy, enthusiasm and compassion to the more important task of helping others find a happier life.

It started during his Navy service in the Pacific during World War II when his ship, a small destroyer escort, was caught in a terrible typhoon while enroute from Okinawa to Leyte Gulf.

During a three-day period, two other identical ships capsized, foundered and sank and their crews were lost.

"The ship I was on," Eby remembers, "was listing 10 to 20 degrees more than it was designed to roll. I started praying and I promised God that if I survived the storm and war I would do whatever He asked me to do."

Floyd remembered that promise and it eventually led him to his present career — trips to communes, prisons, bars, homes . . . anywhere in the country, day or night, wherever people are crying out for help.

"I never help anyone," he asserts, "but I show them where they can get all the help they want — right in the Bible."

———————

THOSE WHO KNOW Floyd best will tell you he never preaches. He listens to people, makes friends with them and then explains how he has found true happiness and success in his own life.

"Calling God's Tower . . . Come In Please!" is really a collection of the many experiences he has encountered in his "new life." It is, in our humble opinion, an exciting story written by a man who has always excited our admiration and respect.

The book, printed and published by the Eagle Printing company here in Coldwater (a first of its kind for that company) is being distributed nationally by the Christian Book Store. It also is available at the printers.

Battle Creek Enquirer and News, 1976

Eby remembers state title

His Coldwater team pressed way to '49 cage crown

COLDWATER — Floyd Eby's dark eyes glistened.

In them, and on his face, were reflections of bygone years.

Memories lingered, focused, then exploded outward, still as fresh as Floyd Eby's outlook on life.

In the tasteful comfort of his home on, appropriately enough, Cardinal Drive just a couple of dribbles away from Coldwater High School, he was reliving things near and dear to him.

Things he cares about. Things that matter to him. In typical Eby fashion, the emphasis was on people. And kids. Especially kids.

"Oh, they've really turned out well," he said, in reference to the members of Coldwater High School's 1949 state championship basketball team — a team he coached to the state title, the only one Coldwater has won.

This year's Cardinal team, under the tutelage of Eby's former student and player Fred Hobart, is pursuing another state title. They play Grand Rapids West Catholic Thursday at 7:30 p.m. in Western Michigan University's Read Fieldhouse. Coldwater won its first regional title since that Eby-coached state champ-

Bob's Beat
with Bob Byington

ionship team last Thursday, bombing Caledonia.

Eby chuckled. "They (his 1949 team) used to work hard and I really used to work them, too. They were really a quick bunch and they were a heady group of kids, too. Yes, they've turned out well. The team members now include an ordained minister, a couple of dentists, a couple of Army officers and several businessmen."

The words were gushing out now. His face brightened. Somehow the stately Victorian furniture that filled the Eby's living room seemed out of place in the midst of all this uninhibited expression.

He looked at the bronze plaque commemorating the state title with the names of the team's players and the results of each game etched on the metal.

"We beat Alma in the quarter-finals, 51-42, that year," he said. "They were rated the number one Class B team in the state at that time. We almost blew it in the semifinal game against Grand Rapids Godwin Heights, though. We barely won, 36-35."

That set up the championship battle between Coldwater and River Rouge, coached by Lofton Greene, now a good friend of Eby's. Greene has since won 12 Class B basketball titles. But he didn't win in 1949. That year belonged to Eby and Coldwater ... and the Cardinals' helter-skelter full-court press.

With that pressure defense and a lot of grit, Coldwater survived, 49-42, capping a 21-2 season.

Gene Sowles, a co-captain on that state championship team, has nurtured a trio of outstanding all-around athletes at Coldwater High School — Tom, Mike and Randy, the quarterback of this year's Cardinal team from his guard position. A fourth Sowles, younger brother Mark, will soon be a high school student.

Eby's starting five that championship season averaged only around 5-9, so it was imperative that they press, press and press some more if they were to survive. All the aggressive, larcenous Cardinals cared about was where and when their next steal or double team could be pulled off.

The press was still a relatively new phenomenon at that time. "After we got out of the districts, very few teams had seen our brand of ball, so we had an advantage," Eby smiled, suddenly turning the clock back 30 years and relishing the moment.

Reportedly, River Rouge's Greene was so impressed with Coldwater's press that he incorporated into his team's style of play the next season. He's never let up on his way to the

12 state titles. Some say Greene gave credit to Eby for introducing him to the press. Eby, with customary self-effacement, pooh-poohs that and says it's bunk.

"He may give me credit for the press, but that's a bunch of baloney," said Eby. "People give me credit for introducing the full-court zone press and the box-and-one zone defense. It's just something I fell into. I certainly didn't devise it because of my intelligence."

Some of his coaching rivals might argue that point. Eby devised a numbering system for his players to make the press easier for them to execute. Each player knew exactly where he was supposed to be at any given time on the press.

"Once a team got through our press, each player had points where they'd race to before the ball or the player with the ball got there," Eby explained. "It was unusual to see players race and run and work that hard on defense. But we'd run back and still get interceptions when the other team thought they had us in a hole."

He was warming up to the subject now. He hunched forward a bit, as I expected he did on the bench when he was coaching. His eyes ignited with a competitive fire. He lurched ahead verbally.

"When they thought they had us, they'd make that one last pass," he said. "And we'd be there to intercept it. Lots of times, once a team thought it had broken our press, they wouldn't make that last pass, they'd shoot the outside jump shot. But they always looked for us because once they broke our press, we'd press 'em again further down the floor. Our defense was an important part of our offense."

To hear Eby tell it, that press defense came about quite by accident when he was a graduate student at Michigan State and the football and basketball coach at Williamston High in 1940.

It was a concession of sorts, a compromise - all to keep his star scorer in the game.

From the very first practice, Eby noticed that one player, the scoring star of the year before, never left the offensive end of the floor. That meant that two opposing players had to be guarded by one of his players.

He knew that wouldn't work. So he devised a 2-2 (box) zone and let his star player chase the opposition player who had the ball. Gradually, this team caught onto the new alignment, moved it down floor. The full-court zone press, an Eby trademark, was born.

Naturally, this speeded up play on both ends of the court. Hence the advent of the one-handed set and jump shots. "Everyone in those days was using the two-handed set shot. We couldn't do that because it took too much time to get set and we were constantly on the move. So, I told our players to jump and throw it up there with one hand like a dog."

He was laughing heartily now, amused at the recollection. "Everyone thought we were crazy and I guess we were." More laughter.

Eby's Williamston team pressed and ran and hustled its way to a state championship in 1940.

Eby coached at Williamston for four years, then came to Coldwater in the fall of 1943. His last year of coaching was in 1964. Then he turned the coaching reins over to Hobart, who was the Twin Valley's leading scorer playing under Eby.

"Fred's a good tactician," said Eby. "He always had a good head on his shoulders and it's carried over into his coaching."

And the ballplayers? "That (Rick) Gates kid - whooo - can he shoot! When he misses, you're surprised. And they have heady guards, too. You've got to have good guards or you don't have a good team."

Eby has seen several of Coldwater's tournament games and thinks the Cardinals have a good chance of winning Thursday's quarterfinal game. "I think if we play a good ball game we'll be in the semifinals. I think the kids will be up."

At least Eby hopes so ("I've got Saturday saved. You betcha I've got tickets to the semifinals").

But he has a speaking engagement Thursday and can't attend the quarterfinal game. He retired from teaching in 1970 to devote full time to religion. He flies his own plane thousands of miles to hundreds of towns each year acting as a speaker, evangelist, missionary, lay witness, counselor and Gideon distributing the Word of God.

His Bible sessions, speaking engagements (many acquired from distribution of a book he has written) and counseling sessions consume at least 100 hours a week. Wise business investments have allowed him to talk full time to people about, as he put it, the "New Way of Life."

Coldwater High School is going to honor Eby Thursday. And it's in a way that he probably appreciates most. The students have requested he speak at their pep assembly. The players on the team want him to lead them in a prayer after the assembly.

No, Floyd Eby won't be there in Read Fieldhouse Thursday night. But, chances are, he'll be there in spirit, rooting for the Cardinals to do it one more time.

That's got to count for a lot.

Floyd Eby
. . . honored in Coldwater

Retired coach is honored in Coldwater

COLDWATER — Floyd Eby, a local businessman and retired athletic coach at Coldwater High School, received the community's Outstanding Citizen Award Saturday night at the annual meeting of the Greater Coldwater Area Chamber of Commerce.

About 250 chamber members and guests attended the event.

The chamber's Woman of the Year Award went to Mrs. Dennis (Geogiana) Holcomb, a housewife of 53 Bonnie Lane, and the Man of the Year Award was presented to Jerry Ford of 53 Bishop Ave., a local Realtor.

Eby was recognized for contributions to the community, particularly to youth, during his many years of residence here.

He was head of the high school athletic department from 1943 to 1968. Before coming here, and while a student at Michigan State University, he served as coach at Williamston. He guided Williamston to a state class C basketball championship in 1940. In 1949 his Coldwater Cardinals captured the state's class B basketball championship.

On retiring in 1968, Eby became active in a number of business ventures, including insurance, real estate, contracting and financing.

He has been active in the field of religion and served as president of the Michigan Gideons for three years. A book on his religious experiences, "Calling God's Tower," was published in 1975.

Also honored at the meeting was the chamber's 1975 president, Lester Wise, president of Southern Michigan National Bank.

How shall we escape, if we
neglect so great a salvation;
which at the first began to
be spoken by the Lord, and
was confirmed unto us by them
that heard Him.
Hebrews 2:3

11

AN EXCITING NEW LIFE
My Own Testimony

"Champions Forever" as a book could end at this point, because I have described through my own experiences what it takes to be a champion in athletics through discipline --- physically and mentally.

Through these you develop a competitive spirit and an unwillingness to give up when the going gets rough. But there is something missing, and that something is spiritual development.

If you discipline your mind and body through athletics, so that your body becomes a temple of the soul, what good is it if there is not also spiritual development? If there is not something of value in this temple? If you can develop all three disciplines, my friends --- physical, mental, and spiritual --- then you can truly be a champion forever.

"Now," you say, "Coach Eby is about to give us a lecture on Christianity."

No way. But I would be less than honest if I didn't tell you about this side of my life, which has become so meaningful to me since I left the world of win-loss records, weekend quarterbacks, and athletic involvement.

My two brothers and sister and I were raised on a farm by my Christian parents, Jesse and Marcia Eby. We were a poor family, materially. I resented this poverty and the fact that I had to go without many things my friends had. Although my parents were Christians, I was not. I was more concerned about accumulating material things for myself. I wanted to be an athletic coach even when I was a young lad; I wanted to be a teacher, a sports announcer, a pilot --- and above all, I wanted to make money.

Although I had heard hundreds of sermons and Sunday school lessons, I had never really taken them seriously. My mother was sick for ten years when I was a small boy and a young teenager, and I prayed on my knees each night that God make her well. He never did. And I hated God for that! My mother passed away when I was a freshman at Michigan State.

Through the years leading up to World War II, I never stopped wanting for material things. I understand why, now. It was because I felt so deprived as a child. But at the same time I wanted, I went to church, I taught Sunday school classes, and once in awhile I read the Bible. I thought I was a Christian headed toward Heaven because of the good life I was living personally, and because of my service to my community and to so many young people, especially athletes.

But it took World War II to make me see myself as I really was. I was a Communications Officer overseas on a Destroyer Escort, and my life, like so many at sea during the war, was in danger many times. There was a lot of time to think. And I began to read the Bible more seriously. I found that I was a lost sinner in spite of my "goodness". And I knew I was outside the protection of God.

However, in attempting to make the Bible practical, and to prove it, I became a confused young man.

Finally, one day I decided to either became an atheist and throw out all of this religious nonsense --- or to accept God for what He says He is. I decided right then to accept each word of God as truth, by faith that God is no liar.

I have not been confused since!

However, when the war was over and after I returned to coaching, spiritual growth came slowly, and sometimes painfully. After my coaching career ended and after I turned fully to business, the Lord blessed me with all the material things I sought. How wonderful it is to be in a country where it is possible for a nobody like me to attain such goals so quickly.

But one day the Lord shook me up. *Galatians 6:7 "Be not deceived, God is not mocked; for whatsoever a man soweth, that shall he also reap."*

I lost $40,000.00 in two business deals within three days.

I immediately asked my Lord, "Why me?" I reminded my Lord that I had been going to church regularly, teaching Sunday school class and giving thousands of dollars each year to my church and other missionaries.

My Lord answered me quickly. "Don't give me any more jazz about that money you are giving me. I want your dedication, time, and talent."

So right then I surrendered my life, time, talent, and money to my Saviour. I have been richly blessed ever since.

* * *

Four Reasons Why I Believe and Know The Bible Is True

The following four reasons are why I believe and know the Bible is true. They really make sense to me now. I pray they will also make sense to you, as belief in the Bible is the key to this wonderful way of life I am telling you about.

The first reason I believe the Bible is true is the fulfilling of prophecies. You see, being a scientist, I believed in science, not the Bible. I now completely believe the Bible. Some top scientists are personal friends of mine, and they too at one time were agnostics or atheists, believing only science and not the Bible. Dr. John Moore from Michigan State

University was an avowed agnostic until 1962. He believed in only science, and thought God, Jesus, and the Bible were nonsense as I did. In 1962, Dr. Moore became a Christian, and three years later in 1965, he was speaking to a group of men about the harmony of the Bible and science. By that time I believed the Bible, and I had taught science for many years. I drove up to Michigan State University to hear him.

Dr. Moore used two illustrations that day that I still remember. "At one time," he said, "science had established the fact that there were just 1,054 stars in the Universe." May I ask you readers if you ever tried counting the stars on a clear night? Well, I have, and I found out that when you get up to 15 or 20 stars, you become confused and mixed up and cannot keep track. I have also attempted to count them while in a planetarium where I used to teach about the sun, moon, and stars. It couldn't be done there either.

So, the scientists found they couldn't count the stars. They had collaborated and went to their experts; the books and charts ... and established the scientific fact of 1,054 stars in the Universe, no more and no less.

But while we scientists had established this fact, God's Word had already recorded in Genesis 15:5 that God compared the number of stars with the seed of people, or millions of people. Also, in Hebrew 11:12, God compared the number of stars with the grains of sand at the seashore. Did you ever try to count the grains of sand when you were swimming on a sandy beach?

You see, friends, when science had established the fact of 1,054 stars, God's Word had already recorded that the stars were too numerous to be counted, and now science agrees with the Bible on this.

Dr. Moore also stated that at one time, science had established the fact that the earth was hung in place by cables. Of course, we laugh at that now, because we know that we place things in orbit and around and around they go with nothing attached thereto. Science at that time knew about gravity, but not about space, so science just knew that the earth had to be hooked to something, or it would fall out of space. After talking with the experts -- checking their books and charts --- we scientists decided that it was a fact that the Earth was hung in space by cables.

However, as we go to Job 26:7 we read that God hangeth the earth up on nothing. God's Word is continuing to prove scientific facts as wrong, and the only time that the Bible and science disagree is when science is wrong! Praise God!

The second reason I believe the Bible, and know that it is true, is because it changes people's lives.

Yes, I was one of those people who used to ridicule matured Christians.

"Look at that religious nut. He has gone nuts on religion. He is a fanatic. He is way out in left field. They ought to lock him up and throw away the key. Man -- is he gone!" I used to say.

However, no matter how much I ridiculed the Christians, in my own mind, I had to admit that something was changing their lives, even though the way He was changing them was distasteful to me at the time.

Then when God came in and changed my life and thousands of my friends' lives, I knew it was for real. So it makes sense that the Bible is true if it has the power to change lives.

The third reason I believe the Bible, and know that it is true, is because God is no liar. When I was overseas I had to make a decision, and as I asked myself this question. "Is God the greatest liar ever created, the greatest phony ever produced, the greatest fake ever brought about -- or does He tell the truth and is He what He claims to be?"

You see God is not like Floyd Eby. I tell the truth most of the time and sometimes I lie. But God is either what He claims He is, or He is the greatest liar ever created.

I decided right then and there that *God is no liar.* From the point of starting, I now could make a simple scientific deduction. If God is no liar, then He tells the truth. If He tells the truth, then God said He wrote the Bible, and then it has to all be true, because God only tells the truth. I believe that there can be a few errors in some translations, but I know there is not one error in the original writings, as God wrote it.

In *II Peter 1:20-21* we read, *"Knowing this first, that no prophecy of the scripture is of any private interpretation. For the prophecy came not at any time by the will of man, but holy men of God spoke as they were moved by the Holy Spirit."*

If you wished to write a book and asked me to type it as you dictated to me. And I typed every word just as you told it to me, who would be the author of the book, you or me? You, of course. I was only the typist. You were the author and you understood everything that you wrote even though someone else might read your book and misunderstand some parts of it.

I believe this is the way that God's Book was written. God told these Holy Men of God just what to put down. In other words, these Holy Men of God -- John, Paul, Peter and all the others -- had no choice but to write down exactly what God spoke to them through His Holy Spirit. If I say that God didn't write the Bible in this way, then I am calling Him a liar, because He said He did.

I used to say that I thought parts of the Bible were true, but other parts were not or could not be. However, this same God who cannot lie and wrote the Bible states in *II Timothy 3:16, "All scripture is given by inspiration of God, and is profitable for doctrine, for reproof, for correction, for instruction in righteousness."* God said, "I wrote it all." The Bible in the original writings has to be true, or none of it is true, because God wrote all of it.

The key to our salvation, our faith, our blessings, and all of God's Promises, are wrapped up in the *fact* that God is no liar. Therefore He tells the truth. Therefore He wrote the Bible. Therefore the Bible has to be true, and we can only rely on His Word for salvation, faith, blessings, and all of God's promises.

The fourth reason I believe the Bible and know that it is true, is that I accept by faith that which I cannot understand.

As you read this, I know many of you are saying to

yourself, "Not me, I want everything proven to me." I could prove everything in the Bible to you if only I could place myself on the same intellectual level as God Almighty who wrote the Book. Of course, this is impossible, so I need to accept the parts of the Bible I cannot understand by Faith, because God said it.

I personally fought this concept for years. I am a scientist, a coach, and a teacher, and I wanted all things proven to me as facts. As I diagrammed new football plays, and every man did his job and blocked his man, we would run for a touchdown every play. But we seldom did, because someone was "goofing off," and would miss his man. But I realize that we used faith in our daily living.

One morning one of my high school students came to me in the hall. "Coach Eby, I have some questions to ask you," she said.

"Wait until you come to my first hour class, Sally," I replied, "and we will discuss your questions then."

When the class started, and I gave the students a reading assignment, I took Sally into my adjacent office, and asked her what I could do to help her. She handed me a sheet of questions, and I quickly looked at them and found the questions to be all anti-God and anti-Christian.

"Did you make up these questions, Sally?"

"No," came the answer, "I got them from my boyfriend at the University."

I thought to myself, this is about "par" for the course.

"This is Friday," I said. "Let me take your questions home over the weekend, and I will look up the answer in God's Word."

The next Monday morning in the hallway, Sally asked if I had the answers to her questions, and I told her I would see her in class. Once again I took her to my office.

"Yes, Sally," I said, "I have some answers to your questions, but you are not going to be satisfied with them."

"Why not?" she asked.

"Because you don't accept the Bible as true and God's Word."

I took the Bible from my desk and held it up. "We must accept the parts of the Bible we can't understand by faith, because God said it."

Sally struck the desk with her fist, and indignantly replied, "You are just like the rest of them. I thought you could help me but you're just like the others, expecting me to accept the Bible on blind faith. I just won't do that because I am not that type of person."

"I am sorry, Sally, that you don't live with your mother," I mentioned.

"But I do," she said.

"No, you don't," I replied.

"Yes, I do."

"No, you don't."

"Yes, I do. You know I do, Coach. You have been to my home and I have introduced you to my mother."

"I regret to inform you, Sally, that is not your real mother. I think you got mixed up in the hospital and were sent to the wrong home."

"I know better than that," Sally protested.

"How do you know, Sally? Did you ever have a blood test? Even that would not prove it for sure."

By now Sally was somewhat confused, and I said to her, "Sure, Sally, you know she is your mother and I know she is your mother, but only through faith that we accept."

Sally saw the point.

Once in a while my teenage daughter would act nasty at home, and sometimes I would say to her, "You know, you are no daughter of mine. My daughter would not act like that. You must have been mixed up in the hospital, and sent to the wrong home." Her mother would answer, "She acts just like her dad."

If I asked you readers who the first President of the United States was, most of you would tell me George Washington. I buy that. In fact, if someone today was able to prove to me that George Washington wasn't the first President of the United States, I would be disturbed. All my life I have known that Washington was the first President.

I wasn't there, and I can't prove it but I believe it. I read it in history books. I would like to ask you the question "Does it make sense to believe without a shadow of a doubt, a history book written by men and women, accepting George Washington as the first President of the United States and many other historical events, and not believe a book (the Bible) written by God? I am sure your answer is, that if we are to accept history books by faith, we must accept the Bible by Faith!

In summary, I believe that the Bible is true, because of the fulfilling of prophecies; because it changes peoples' lives; because God is no liar, and He said He wrote the Bible, and because I accept those parts of the Bible I cannot understand by faith because God said it.

This makes sense to me and I am sure it does to you. If it does make sense to you, then the scriptures can show you as they showed me, the way to join the Family of God.

God Shows The Way

Since we now believe and know that the Bible is true, God will show us through four verses of scripture how to join the Family of God. The first verse is *Romans 3:23.* *"For all have sinned, and come short of the Glory of God."*

For many years I have thought this verse included everyone except Floyd Eby. One day I realized that the "all" in the English langugage means everybody but Jesus, and that includes all evangelists, all preachers, all men, all women, all children, and most of all, it included me.

You see, I don't know one bad thing about you and you don't know anything bad about me, because we don't know each other. But as you read this book, you know that Floyd Eby does some wrong. You know that much without even knowing me, because God says in this verse that all do wrong, and that not only has to include me, but you, too.

Therefore, you and I are in the same boat. We both do wrong and we need help. In fact, we need the Saviour.

Another important truth of this verse is that it takes any

right away from me to criticize your way of living. If I criticize the things you do, then I am judging you for the same things I do. You might wonder if I do the same wrong things you do. Maybe not, but God says I do wrong, and wrong is wrong. I have all I can do to keep my relationship between me and Jesus in proper condition, without judging you.

The second verse is *Romans 6:23*. *"For the wages of sin is death, but the gift of God is eternal life through Jesus Christ our Lord."* Sometimes, we get all mixed up in terminology. You've heard of people becoming Christians, having eternal life, everlasting life, going to Heaven, being born again, being saved, and joining the Family of God. I have heard people say that they are one of the above, but not another, and so on.

But according to the scriptures, the terms all mean the same thing. The terms I like to use is that when I took the necessary steps by faith in Jesus, I joined the Family of God. This makes all Christians brothers and sisters in Christ.

In order to receive a gift, three facts have to be present. First, the gift has to be free. Second, the giver has to be willing to give it. And Third, the recipient has to be willing to receive it. It cannot be a gift unless all of these facts are present.

If I told you I was going to give you a Bible, but I never did, it would never become a gift. If I charged you even ten cents for it, it would not be a gift because you paid for it. Therefore, it wasn't free.

On the other hand, I could be willing to give you this Bible free, and you could say, "Take your Bible, Eby, and keep it. I don't want it." It would never become a gift because you had exercised your right to reject it.

God has a free gift that He wants to give every one of us, but we have the right to accept it or reject it. If we don't accept it, then we reject it. Even though God wants all of us to have it, He will not force it on us, because He has given each of us a free choice.

You see, friends, we have a wonderful God. He has so set up His plan for our lives that no one has to go to Heaven if he doesn't want to. Isn't that wonderful? Because God gave Floyd Eby a choice, and I rejected it for many years, I should not force my beliefs on anyone else who isn't willing to read or listen.

In fact, I always tell people that as I am talking to them about Jesus, if they don't want to hear it, just say so, and I will turn off. This is God's Way.

The third verse is *John 1:12*. *"But as many as received Him, to them gave He power to become the children of God, even to them that believe on his Name."* We have our choice, but if we do accept His gift, we immediately become a child of God.

I was brought up in a poor family on a farm in poverty conditions. What money we had, most of it had to go for my mother's doctor and hospital bills. I could not have the things that my friends had.

I couldn't even have a used bicycle, much less a car. I had to work when the other boys could play ball. I resented this poverty, and vowed I was going to do something about it.

You see, my mother and father loved me, but they were limited in what they could do for me because of the lack of material substance.

I sometimes wished that I had been born to a different Mom and Dad, so I could have the things somes of my friends had. I realize now how foolish it was for my childish mind to think this way, but you see, my parents had limitations.

But when I joined the Family of God, God became my Heavenly Father, and He has no limitations like my earthly Mom and Dad had. My Heavenly Father owns the whole world and everything in it, and there is nothing he cannot do.

He can give me health or He can let me lose it. He has done both in my lifetime. He can give me wealth or He can let me lose it. He has done both in my lifetime. He can keep my plane aloft, or let it crash. Praise God, He has done only one so far. It was, and still is, a real thrill to join a family with a father with whom all things are possible.

The fourth verse is *Revelation 3:20*. *"Behold, I stand at* the door, and knock, if any man hear my voice, and open the door, I will come in to him, and will sup with him, and he with me." Since we know that God wrote the Bible, and that Jesus is God on the earth, then we know as we read the verse Revelation 3:20, it is actually Jesus speaking to you and me.

As I talk with people all over the United States, I find that the great "hang-up" on Christianity is all the Do's and Don'ts that churches, ministers, and other Christians throw at people. But I find that God and His Word does not do this. There is absolutely nothing we have to do to acquire salvation. When Jesus spoke to me overseas He didn't say, "Floyd, I stand at the door and knock. If you quit cheating on your income tax, quit smoking, quit drinking, quit using drugs, quit swearing, quit running around on your wife, quit gambling, quit dancing, and hear my voice and invite me in, I will come in."

No, Jesus didn't put any conditions to my accepting Him as my Saviour and joining the Family of God, except to invite Him into my life, and believe and have faith that He will come in.

All Jesus said was, "Floyd, I stand at the door and knock, and if you hear my voice and invite me in, I will come in, and you will become my child."

Jesus is no liar. He will do just that. Jesus is not talking about the front doors of our houses, but about our bodies. He says that He is ready at any time to send His Holy Spirit into our bodies and lives, and make us children of God, if we just invite Him in and mean it!

My Decision to Receive Christ As My Saviour

Confessing to God that I am a sinner, believing that the Lord Jesus died for my sins on the cross, and was raised for my justification, I do now receive and confess Him as my personal Saviour.

When I was overseas, in the United States Navy, at the age of 26, I took the three necessary steps, according to the Scriptures, and joined the Family of God.

To take *Step One:* I had to promise God that when He told me I am displeasing Him, I would come to Him, and be truly sorry and ask for His forgiveness, and He would forgive me. Please notice only God can tell me what I am doing wrong. Only He has the right to judge me. You have no right because you are a sinner also.

Also, please notice that I do not have to tell any evangelist, minister, friend, relative, counselor, psychiatrist, or even my wife. I only have to tell Jesus, and He already knows, so that is no big deal, and did not present a problem to me. I sincerely promised Jesus that I would do this.

Step Two: I have to believe that Jesus, who is God upon the earth, died on the cross for your sins and my sins. Now, I don't understand this at all, but there is one part of it that I can understand. That is how Jesus can love you and me enough to give up His life for us, if that is the way He wants to do it.

I am sure if you have a son or daughter, and they were out in the street, and a huge truck was going to run over them, you would rush out to the street, and push them out of the way of the truck -- even though it meant losing your own life.

You would say, "Yes, I would do that because of my love for my children." However, I could offer you a million dollars to lay down in front of a large truck and be squashed to death, and you would turn the proposition down. You wouldn't sacrifice your life for money but you would for love. I would do the same for my daughters.

Now, if this is true of you and me, then we have to admit if we can love that much, then we know that Jesus, who is Divine, is capable of much greater love than you or I. So, certainly we can understand how He can love us enough to give up His life for us if that is the way He wants it.

I still don't understand how being nailed to the cross, crucified, and the shedding of His blood paid for my sins. But I don't have to understand, because He stated in the Bible that He wrote, that is the way He did it, and remember God is no liar!

Step Three: I have to believe that after Jesus was crucified and died on the cross, He was taken down and put in a tomb. Three days later He arose from the dead. Now, I don't understand how God did this, but I do know that God states four times in the Old Testament and four times in the New Testament in different words but all meaning the same thing: *that with God all things are possible -- and God is no liar!*

God wrote the Bible, and He said He arose from the dead, and so I believe it.

Salvation is *simple, sure, and complete.* We must promise God that we will be truly sorry for our sins, we must believe that Jesus died on the cross for our sins, and that three days later Jesus arose from the dead for our justification. If we really mean it when we say to Jesus that we do believe, accept, and actually receive these three steps into our being as truth and by faith, then according to the scriptures, you and I are truly children of God and have joined the Family of God. We are truly brothers and sisters in Christ!

Congratulations on the greatest, most profitable, and wonderful decision you have ever made. God loves you and me, and I love you, sister and brother!

> *"But grow in grace, and in the*
> *knowledge of our Lord and Saviour*
> *Jesus Christ. To Him be glory*
> *both now and forever, Amen"*
> *2 Peter 3:18*

12

HOW TO COME ALIVE

Since we now have joined the Family of God, what a wonderful, exciting, and tremendous adventure we have waiting for us.

God's Word is full of promises which He is anxiously waiting to fulfill for each one of His children. We now can expect to look forward to a life filled with exciting and wonderful events each and every day. We can look forward with anticipation to every new day, which can, and will be better than the day before.

I personally have been endowed with all of the secular things of this world we all seek -- even before I joined the Family of God.

I was fortunate to have an excellent job in a wonderful profession, a wonderful family, much publicity, community status, a beautiful home, new cars, my own plane, many friends, successful businesses, money, state basketball championships, football and baseball championships, and many other honors during my short lifetime.

However, even though many of these accomplishments were exciting and thrilling, each one eventually became routine.

The new cars were great. But I didn't wash them much after the first month, and they soon faded into routine transportation.

The glow of athletic championships soon grew dim, and faded into just pleasant memories.

The making of money became an obsession that didn't leave time for the better things of life. The beautiful new home and swimming pool were wonderful, but soon became commonplace.

Becoming a successful business executive was a real boost to my ego, but presented many problems in living a happy, fruitful life. The publicity and honors made me feel important, but all were soon forgotten. When I first flew my own plane all by myself, I thought this was it. The ultimate. But it, too, became just a good way to travel.

All of the above became routine until I joined the Family of God, and I started using the above accomplishments to serve my Saviour. The only part of my life that never becomes routine is my personal relationship with the Lord Jesus. As I know Him better and better, every day gets better and better, and my relationship with Jesus is sweeter each and every day.

After we join the Family of God, Jesus only asks us to become His close friend. Another way of putting it is to grow spiritually, get closer to God, get to know Him better and better, putting God first, or increasing our faith. Jesus doesn't give us do's and don'ts. He just tells us how to become His close friend, and He will take care of everything else.

Each child of God is handled as a special case by Jesus. Our own relationship with Jesus has nothing to do with anybody else. He holds us responsible according to our spiritual age.

Let's say you are one year old, and you are walking. You

trip over your mom's best lamp and smash it. Your mother doesn't beat the tar out of you, because you are not old enough to know better. If you did it a few years later on purpose, she would let you know in no uncertain terms that it was wrong.

You see, friends, we hold our children responsible according to their chronological age, and the law also holds us responsible to some degree according to our age. But God holds us responsible according to our spiritual age, and all of us may be at different spiritual ages or levels.

How do I know this? Because there are things I could do a couple of years ago that were all right between me and my Saviour that I cannot do now, because I am now closer to God, and older spiritually.

Many times when dope addicts and alcoholics join the Family of God, the first question they ask is, "Do I have to give up my dope and alcohol now?"

I always reply, "You don't have to give up anything."

"What did you say?" they will ask.

"I said, you don't have to give up anything. Just make friends with Jesus. He will change your life at the accepted time, and you don't have to give up anything. He will take it away from you and make it a blessing."

"Each of us is too weak to give up things, but God is strong. God will strengthen us through the Holy Spirit as we put Him first in our lives, and our lives will then change. I know it, because that is how God is changing my life."

After I became a Christian, I still played poker with my coaching friends. It was a small friendly game where you lose or win five or ten dollars during the evening. At the time it wasn't wrong between me and my Jesus to play poker, as He didn't speak to me about it.

However, as I grew spiritually, Jesus started speaking to me. He let me know that it wasn't a very good example to my coaching friends, and might instead be a stumbling block to their own personal encounter with Jesus.

I spoke back to the Lord, "Lord I love to play poker, and I am not going to give it up."

As I continued to play each week, my leadings from the Lord became stronger. I finally rationalized that playing poker wasn't bad. It was winning that was bad. I decided I would continue to play poker, but I would make sure that I would not win. However, I didn't want to lose very much so I played it close to my belt, and tried to lose only a dollar or so.

I played three more weeks and I won each time. The only time I had ever been a consistent winner. I still refused to stop playing. I rationalized that playing poker wasn't bad, and winning wasn't bad, but taking the winnings home was bad. So when I would leave the game about midnight, I would take my winnings, put them in the next pot and tell my friends to play for them.

"Take your filthy earnings home, Eby. We don't want your filthy money. Take it, and forget it," they would remark sarcastically.

I would tell them I didn't want their money, and I would leave. After a couple of weeks of this, on my way home I thought, "Here I am fighting God on this, and even making my best friends mad at me." That was the last of my poker playing.

You see, I didn't give it up, but God took it away from me, and made it a real blessing. I no longer had God on my back, or my friends mad at me, and my wife was real happy. I felt good, and what a blessing it was to please Jesus.

However, I am not saying it is wrong for other Christians if you gamble. It is wrong for a Christian to do anything that is displeasing to Jesus. He will let us know when we displease Him, and this will continually change as we grow spiritually.

The important question is how to grow spiritually -- how to know Him better and better -- how to get closer to God -- how to put God first -- how to increase our faith -- how to become a real close friend of Jesus?

When I first meet someone, I may decide that I really like this guy, and I want to become a real close friend of his. This would be impossible if I decided that I never wanted to see him again, never wrote to him, never telephoned him, or visited him. We would feel that such actions would be stupid, if we were really trying to be close friends.

On the same basis, we cannot become a close friend of Jesus if we refuse to read about Him in His Bible, refuse to talk to Him in prayer, refuse to be with His people, and refuse to serve Him.

To become a close friend of Jesus, or to grow spiritually, or to get to know Him better, or to be closer to God, or to put Him first, or to increase our faith, we need to follow Jesus' commands to: 1. *Read the Bible,* 2. *Talk with God,* 3. *Be with other Christians,* 4. *Serve Jesus.*

Read the Bible

Till I come, give attendance to reading"
1 Timothy 4:13a
"Study to show thyself approved unto God,
a workman that needeth not to be ashamed,
rightly dividing the word of truth."
2 Timothy 2:15

Many people after they have joined the Family of God (I have encouraged them to read the Bible) have come back and told me they were having trouble understanding it.

I answer, "Hallelujah! Join the crowd. There are many things in the Bible I can't understand either. But God doesn't tell me that I must understand it; just that I must read or hear it."

If we do read or hear it, our Lord will reveal truths to us as we are ready for these truths, and He will bless our lives. However, if we refuse to read or hear it, He will not bless our lives by revealing truths from His Word.

You and I could read the same chapter at the same time, and perhaps God would reveal a truth to you and not to me, because you are ready for that truth, and I am not yet ready.

The things in the Bible that I can't understand do not bother me. It is the things that I do understand that I have trouble with, and many truths in the Bible are very simple and easy to understand. I therefore have no excuse before Jesus when I displease Him by not following His guidelines for my life.

The real fundamental necessary truths needed for my salvation and spiritual growth were recorded in the Bible several times, in simple language, by several different Holy Men of God as they were directed by the Spirit of God.

Such fundamental beliefs as the Virgin Birth, the Crucifixion, The Resurrection, the Second Coming, and the belief that the Bible is God's Holy Inspired Word, are true and accurate because the original recordings were written by God Himself.

Controversial doctrine is important to us and to our numerous different denominations. I am sure it pleases God for us to join with other Christians in a local fellowship of like faith and doctrine to promote the cause of Jesus.

However, I believe there are only two groups when it comes to spirituality. Either we are believers or unbelievers. And if we are not believers, we are unbelievers. It is important that we love the Lord Jesus Christ, and accept in faith the fundamental truths necessary to join the Family of God according to the Scriptures.

I believe much misunderstanding comes from the term "church" in the Bible. When God uses the term "church" in His Bible, I believe He is referring to a group of believers gathering for the purpose of worshipping our Lord.

This can include all of the different denominations, organizations, church buildings, missionary groups, broadcasting, television, home Bible studies, prayer meetings, meetings in cars, planes, or on the job. I don't believe our Lord would just have us equate the biblical term church with a denominational organization and a church building.

We need to read the Bible daily, and the more we read, the more our Jesus will bless us with the truths needed to live a happy, fruitful life.

Talk With God

In the Bible, God commands us to talk or pray to Him. *I Timothy 2:8 "I will, therefore, that men pray everywhere, lifting up holy hands, without wrath and doubting."*

I Thessalonians 5:17 "Pray without ceasing." Acts 6:4 "But we will give ourselves continually to prayer, and to the ministry of the Word." Luke 18:1 "And He spoke a parable unto them to this end, that men ought always to pray, and not to faint."

To become a close friend of anyone, we need to talk and visit with them. The same is true if we become a close friend to Jesus; we need to talk and visit with Him, which many call prayer. We can talk to Him in public or in private, on our knees, or in any position, out loud or without utterance, at any time, and at any place, and about any thing. To grow spiritually, we need to talk to God many times a day, and He will bless us for it!

Let us not forget to praise Him and pray for others as well as ourselves.

Be With Other Christians

The Bible commands us to join in fellowship with believers, and people of like faith. *Acts 2:42 "And they continued steadfastly in the apostles' doctrine and fellowship, and in breaking of bread, and in prayers." I John 1:3 "That which we have seen and heard declare we unto you, that ye also may have fellowship with us; and truly our fellowship is with the Father, and with His Son, Jesus Christ." I John 1:7 "But if we walk in the light, as He is in the light, we have fellowship one with another, and the blood of Jesus Christ, His Son cleanseth us from all sin."*

You would probably like to ask me if I ever associate with unbelievers? I certainly do. I have hundreds of coaching friends who believe just as I do. I also have hundreds of friends who do not believe as I do. I have spent many a night talking basketball and football with coaching friends who were not Christians.

I enjoyed these evenings very much, and there is not anything wrong with it. However, I have to admit that when

I am with my unbelieving friends, nothing happens to get me closer to the Lord.

In fact, I am drawn away from God. So you see, I need to spend the majority of my time with other people of like faith if I want to become a closer friend of Jesus, grow spiritually, get to know Him better, and better, or increase my faith.

Christian people surrounding us with their presence, their compassion, concern, and love, will have a real influence on our spiritual growth. We have to be real strong spiritually, to keep an environment of unbelievers from dragging us away from our God.

What are some of the ways to obtain the needed Christian fellowship? Following is a suggested list: churches and other Christian Service Organizations, Christian friends, home Bible studies, Christians meetings, retreats, and conferences, your own program of serving Jesus, Christian Schools, Christian parties, Christian excursions, the making of your own home into a place of Christian gatherings.

Serve Jesus

We are commanded by the Bible to obey and serve Jesus. *John 12:26 "If any man serve me, let him follow me; and where I am, there shall also my servant be; if any man serve me, him will my Father honour." Colossians 3:23, 24 "And whatsoever ye do, do it heartily, as to the Lord, and not unto men." "Knowing that of the Lord ye shall receive the reward of the inheritance; for ye serve the Lord Christ." Ephesians 6:7 "With good will doing service, as to the Lord, and not to men."*

When we start serving Jesus through His leading, we will really grow rapidly spiritually and get close to God. As we serve Him regularly, we will become His best friend, and He will shower us with abundant blessings. I don't know how God will have you serve Him, but I do know that if we grow spiritually, He will tell us how He would have us serve Him.

I am sure God would have you serve Him differently than He has me. All I can do is tell you what doors of service He has opened for me: Giving messages about the Bible and my Lord at banquets, churches, schools, clubs, conferences and conventions; a witnessing and personal follow-up program; my church and many other service organizations; home Bible studies, television programs, jail ministry; counseling couples with marital trouble; counseling alcoholics, dope addicts, and law violators concerning help from God and the Bible; writing Christian books, and through other avenues of service.

God has opened so many doors that now it is thrilling to watch how He can guide me into new service by closing doors in present service. I can sincerely say that I have never been any happier than I am now when He has opened so many doors through which I can walk and receive real blessings. Praise His Holy Name!

Family Devotions

God will bless any family of believers who will designate a time each day and have a devotional period with all members of the family present. When you have it, during the day or night, will depend on the time necessary to have everyone present. Our devotional period is in the morning before breakfast, and consists of the reading of a portion of God's Word, an illustration about the reading, prayer requests, and prayer.

We know that forty per cent of all marriages today end up in divorce. But recent surveys taken of thousands of families who are Christians, go to church and other Christian meetings together, have daily devotions, read the Bible together daily, pray together daily, and take their problems to the Lord, indicate that only one out of 900 such marriages end up in divorce.

I am sure you will agree that there is no marriage counselor, psychologist, psychiatrist, minister, or anyone else who can bring about such results. But God's precious Holy Inspired Word, the Bible, and the Holy Spirit can.

* * *

Through my many years of working with all kinds of people with problems, I have found only one solution: The Bible and God. I have also found that 90 per cent of the people have "hang-ups" on Christianity, preachers, churches, Christians, and the Bible, because of all of the do's and don'ts that all the Christians have thrown at them.

They have been told they would have to do this and not be able to do that. You must not smoke, drink, use dope, dance, play cards, wear mini-skirts, commit adultery, swear, steal, etc. I call this a list of "things."

I sincerely believe that no minister ever changed a person's life by preaching "things" from the pulpit. God's Word put no restrictions or do's and don'ts in joining the Family of God. We need to preach and teach Jesus Christ and His Word in every temple and every house.

As a person joins the Family of God and then grows spiritually under the preaching and teaching of Jesus Christ, then that person will have his life changed by the removal of the "things" by God at the accepted time.

Home Bible Studies

Acts 5:42 "And daily in the temple, and in every house, they ceased not to teach and preach Jesus Christ." I believe that we have attempted to spread the News of a Wonderful Saviour in the wrong way. We have established beautiful church buildings, hired articulate preachers, trained Sunday School teachers, organized our churches and Sunday schools to the utmost, purchased buses, and had evangelistic meetings.

We have then waited for the unsaved to come in, or have contests to draw them in or have calling programs to try and get them to the church. I am not saying that the above methods are wrong, but we have to admit the methods listed have not produced enough of the desired results.

Jesus traveled to where people were. He did not stay in

one place and wait for people to show up. Jesus said, "Go, Ye." I believe we have to follow the example of Jesus; we need to go to where the people are.

We need to go into homes; not to invite them to church, but to tell them about Jesus. We can "beat" a person over the head enough, and get him to church even two Sundays in a row. Then he stays home the third Sunday, and we have to start all over again.

Why should an unsaved person enjoy coming to church or to evangelistic meetings? Did you, before you were saved? We need to visit people in their own surroundings and explain salvation to them.

Once they have joined the Family of God, and start growing in the Word, most of them will then want to come to church to be fed in the Word by our ministers, have fellowship with God's Children, and want to serve Jesus.

We need to go to the homes, hippie communes, jails, hospitals, sanitariums, schools, civic clubs, and any other place that God opens up, and talk to people about Jesus and the Bible. We need to talk to people we work with, on breaks and at noon hours. We need to talk to them on the street, or during recreation whenever God opens a door.

People who will never attend a church will allow you to come to their home, if approached properly under God's Guidance, to talk with them about the Bible and Jesus and this new way of life. Neighbors will also come to your own home to read and discuss the Bible if you invite them. The home Bible study should be voluntary and permit free will in every aspect.

Don't "bug" people if they miss; just keep inviting them. Be available, and pray for them, and let them know that you are praying for them. No one reads unless they choose to. Don't ask questions of specific individuals unless you are sure they are willing. Just throw the question out to the group. Let them comment or give illustrations if they desire.

Don't put anyone on the spot. Be simple in your teaching. Give them milk until they are ready for the meat. Teach the fundamental necessities of joining the Family of God and growing spiritually. Don't argue controversial doctrine. Emphasize the importance of loving the Lord Jesus, and do not push your own convictions down other people's throats.

God gave each one of us a choice, and we have no right to insist that others agree with us.

The length of the Bible study will depend on the people involved, conditions, and God's leading.

However, none of them should "drag". In one home I only spend from five to ten minutes, reading a few verses of scripture, make a few comments, ask for their prayer requests, and close in prayer. On the other hand, I have a home Bible study that lasts 90 minutes. Between these two extremes are many others with varying times.

Every new person should, within a few weeks, if not the same night, be taken through the scriptures, have God's Plan for his or her life explained, and be given the opportunity to make a decision. Of course this is dependent on their desire to do so.

Be sure to make friends first. Don't talk "things" or problems; just talk Jesus and how to join His Family; how to get close to Him. Encourage people to get close to Him by reading the Bible, talking with Jesus, being with other Christians, and serving Jesus. All other "things" are up to God.

Discipline

We must discipline ourselves to grow spiritually and get close to God. It takes discipline on our part to do the things necessary to come close to God. It takes discipline to read the Bible daily, to pray daily, to be with Christians, and to serve Jesus.

Many times there is other literature I would rather read than the Bible, but I know that the Bible only can give me a happy, fruitful life. So I must set a time aside daily to read the Bible even if I would rather not.

It takes discipline to pray daily especially when everything is going well. It is easy to spend time in prayer when we have problems like illness that we cannot handle. How much time do we spend talking to God when we don't have problems? God said, "Pray without ceasing."

It takes discipline to be with other Christians. It might seem to be more fun to skip that Christian meeting and go to the ball game or go bowling, but our real happiness depends on fellowship of Christians to give us strength, and assurance for a really happy way of life.

It takes discipline to serve Jesus when He calls us or leads us to serve Him. Sometimes, I would rather sit at home than to make a needed call. I am tired and weary, but fatigue is mainly of the mind, and the joy of serving Jesus will completely rest us.

When we are completely exhausted over a period of time, God is able and will give us time to recover. Many times I have reached this point, and God has downed me and my plane with bad weather for a day or two. I come back home completely rested. Our Wonderful Saviour knows and understands all of our needs.

Commitment

How can we have all our prayers answered? How can we have all the bad things that happen to us turn out good? How can we have all of God's promises fulfilled in our lives? I sincerely believe that all of the above can be fulfilled in all of the believers' lives.

It can happen to each of us as we simply covenant with our Lord Jesus to make and keep a deep commitment to continually strive to put God first in our lives at all times!

I am married to a wonderful woman named Betty. This marriage has lasted 38 years. If I put four other women ahead of my wife in our marriage, it will not be a satisfactory marriage relationship. In fact if you know my Betty, if I put one woman ahead of her, it will not be a good marriage.

The only way that I can have a satisfactory marriage relationship with my wife is by putting her the top woman in my life, and for her to put me the top man in her life. At the present time that is what both of us are doing and we have a wonderful marriage relationship.

But what about our relationship with God? Can we put four other things in our lives ahead of our God, or twenty, or fifty, or even one, and have a successful relationship with Him?

I believe the answer is simple. If my wife won't tolerate anything but being first in my life, my God won't either! Therefore, if I want a blessed, happy, fruitful life, I need to put my God first!

I am sure you readers are thinking, "Coach, do you always put God first in your life?" I have to admit to you that I don't. I am also weak. But I can honestly tell you that when I do, great things happen in my life, and when I don't, things get sticky and messy.

I would like to point out to you three verses of scriptures. *Psalm 37:5 "Commit thy way unto the Lord; trust also in Him; and He shall bring it to pass."*

What is God really saying to me? I believe He is telling me, "Coach, live a life pleasing to me and put me first in your life, then take every problem you have, health, family problems, finances, jobs, etc. and place them all into my hands and forget them as I will take care of them!" God said that. God is no liar, and if I put Him first in my life He will take care of everything.

Romans 8:28 "And we know that all things work together for good to them that love God, to them who are the called according to His purpose."

I know that according to Revelation I am not to add or subtract from the scriptures, but for my own use I paraphrase the above verse: All things work out to good for those who love God, if I love Him enough to put Him first in my life. Then it works for me.

Revelation 21:4 "And God shall wipe away all tears from their eyes; and there shall be no more death, neither sorrow, nor crying, neither shall there be any more pain; for the former things are passed away."

In this verse, God has indicated that He has the right to use us believers any way that He desires while we are upon this earth, because He has guaranteed our future for eternity!

If I told you that if you would work for me just one hour in a terrible job, but it wouldn't kill you and it wasn't dishonest, I would promise you all the money you could spend during the rest of your life time on this earth, I am sure you would say, "Lead me to that job Coach, I can stand anything for one hour to insure my entire future financially."

Friends that is what God is telling us, "Children, if you will just let me use your lives while on this earth anyway I want to, and to my Glory, I will insure your future for eternity, forever and forever."

Do we realize that one hour compared to a life time of even seventy years is much, much more time than seventy years compared to eternity!

Please God help me to praise and thank you no matter what happens to me on this earth, because you have promised me the future forever with no problems.

How Christians Can Help Others

Nearly all people need help, believers and unbelievers alike. As Christians we need to help people. We need to be willing under God's Guidance to spend our time, material substance, and talent. However, I am convinced that though we need to be concerned about peoples' physical needs, we never really are of any real help unless we include the spiritual needs.

In my humble opinion, there are three things that we believers can do for unbelievers, and back sliding believers. *The first is to pray for them even when we don't want to. Second, we need to get as close to God as we possibly can ourselves.* Remember, people are watching us and will see how God is changing our life. This can have more influence on others than anything else. *Thirdly, don't ever "bug" other people, just love them!* Criticism turns people off, but they cannot resist or fight the love of Jesus.

As I counsel with people who are children of God, I suggest they go on a spiritual program for 60 days, and then evaluate the results. The spiritual program I suggest is as follows:

1. Daily Bible reading.
2. Frequent communication with God each day.
3. Daily devotionals with the family or by themselves.
4. Consistent attendance at a church of their choice.
5. A weekly Bible study with friends.
6. Consistent fellowship with other Christians.
7. Serve our Lord Jesus as He directs.

I have yet to know a believer who sincerely followed the above program without finding the power of God's life in solving their problems. On the other hand, we believers who do not follow God's program for our life will not receive help from Him!

When a prison inmate professes Jesus, I encourage him to come to me as soon as he is released from jail. I will then give him the above spiritual program. I notify him that if he follows the spiritual program consistently that God will guarantee that he will never go back to jail. And if he doesn't follow it, I will guarantee that he will go back to jail. That is the way it works out.

For example, when I find Charlie back in jail, I say to him: "Congratulations, Charlie."

"What for?" he will ask.

"For being back in jail," I reply.

"Are you crazy, Coach? I didn't want to come back to jail," he will protest.

"Yes you did," I will insist. "You asked God to put you back in jail and He gave you your wish."

"What makes you say that Coach?"

"Well Charlie, how long did you stay on that spiritual program?"

"Two weeks," he replies.

"When did you come back to jail, Charlie?"

"The third week," he admits.

"You see Charlie, you asked God to put you back into jail when you quit following His Spiritual Program for your life, and He granted your request."

HOW TO COME ALIVE/233

However, friend, the prison inmate is no different than you and I as believers. When we go off of God's Spiritual Program for our lives, we are asking for problems that will mess up our lives, and we are granted our request.

I personally have compassion for all believers who are helpless physically, mentally, and emotionally. I will spend time to help them in any way I can. However, this is a very small group, as most people can help themselves in some way.

I also have compassion for those believers who can help themselves and are trying to do so. I will spend all the time that my Lord will make possible to help them.

The largest group of believers is made up of people who can help themselves, but will not make an effort to do so. I still love this group and will continue to pray for them.

But I will not waste the Lord's time trying to help believers who will not attempt to go on the spiritual program, or make a sincere effort to consistently follow it. *I am wasting my time and the Lord's time if I try to help people who will not lift a finger to help themselves to follow God's Program for their lives.*

Remember, believer, the devil can give us fun, but only God can give us joy. Fun is only temporary, but joy is lasting. Don't seek fun from the devil that creates so many problems for us, but seek joy from Jesus which will solve our problems.

Believer, don't be discouraged when God doesn't take all our bad habits from us. I sincerely believe that each one of us will have a "thorn" that we will have to always battle with. The Apostle Paul did, and God never took it away from him.

If our Lord took all the problems away from us, we would not need Him any more. We are always going to be dependent on God. Believers don't criticize other people's "thorns." Perhaps their "thorn" shows and ours doesn't, but God sees all "thorns."

* * *

While most of this book has been about my athletic career, and about the development of athletes, by now you can see that every person can be a champion -- forever -- by becoming a member of the Family of God.

DATE DUE

GAYLORD			PRINTED IN U.S.A.